W9-BEJ-878

EVERGREEN PILOT BOOKS

Chief Editor
A. Norman Jeffares

Advisory Editors
David Daiches   C. P. Snow

DYLAN THOMAS

DYLAN THOMAS

T. H. Jones

GROVE PRESS, INC.
NEW YORK

CONTENTS

ACKNOWLEDGMENTS

For permission to quote from Dylan Thomas's works, acknowledgments are due to J. M. Dent & Sons Ltd, David Higham Associates Ltd, New Directions, and Putnam & Co. Ltd.

Acknowledgments are also due to Barrie & Rockliffe Ltd (Rayner Heppenstall: *Four Absentees*); the British Council (G. S. Fraser: *Dylan Thomas*); J. M. Dent & Sons Ltd and Little, Brown and Company (John Malcolm Brinnin: *Dylan Thomas in America*); Penguin Books Ltd and John Lehmann (John Lehmann: *New Writing in Europe*); University of Chicago Press (Elder Olson: *The Poetry of Dylan Thomas*); Glyn Jones; Richard Hughes; Vernon Watkins; The Bishop Gore School, Swansea; The Library, University College of Swansea; the *Western Mail*; J. Alexander Rolph; Marie Tietze; Clive Hart.

The photograph on the front cover is reproduced by permission of Radio Times Hulton Picture Library.

for
Sian, Rhiannon, and Ruth Myfanwy

ABBREVIATED TITLES
BY WHICH DYLAN THOMAS'S WORKS ARE CITED

Adventures	=	*Adventures in the Skin Trade.*
C.P.	=	*Collected Poems.*
D.D.	=	*The Doctor and the Devils.*
D.E.	=	*Deaths and Entrances.*
Letters	=	*Letters to Vernon Watkins.*
Portrait	=	*Portrait of the Artist as a Young Dog.*
Prospect	=	*A Prospect of the Sea.*
Q.E.O.M.	=	*Quite Early One Morning.*
Tedlock	=	*Dylan Thomas: The Legend and the Poet*, ed. E. W. Tedlock.
U.M.W.	=	*Under Milk Wood.*

CHAPTER I

THE LOVELY GIFT OF THE GAB

With the possible exception of Ezra Pound, Dylan Thomas may fairly be called the most sensational poet of our time. Thomas achieved early, perhaps too early, fame or notoriety as a poet; and not merely as a poet, but as some sort of Heaven-sent or White-Goddess-given reply, rejoinder, or antistrophe, to what many poetry-starved people felt to be the desolation and aridity of *The Waste Land*, the early *Cantos* of Pound, and the pyloned versions of these in the early poems of those writers whom Roy Campbell cruelly, but not altogether unfairly, lumped together in a savage christening as Macspaunday. Thomas became a legend for reasons which are, perhaps, more connected with the structure of our society than with poetry itself. He went on to achieve another kind of fame through the mass-medium of the radio. Throughout the hectic two decades between the day he caught a train from Swansea to London and the day he died in New York, he had been wildly (and usually unintelligently) acclaimed as a genius, and superiorly denounced as, at worst, a charlatan, at best a young man (from the provinces) with a certain, but terribly ill-trained, and ill-directed talent. Finally, he died, in another country, all too young, and in sordidly dramatic circumstances. It could be said, justifiably, that fate, modern publicity, and Dylan Thomas himself, conspired to raise as many barriers as possible between the sympathetic reader of poetry and the actual poetry that Dylan Thomas wrote.

Thomas was born in Swansea in 1914—a terrible year, as he might have said, taking the words out of the mouths

of his townsmen. No account of the man and the poet
would be complete that did not attempt to convey some
idea of the environment in which he grew up: Swansea,
and what the Welsh know as West Wales, are as important, as fundamental, to Dylan Thomas as Oxford,
Mississippi, to William Faulkner, Dublin to James Joyce,
or Wessex to Thomas Hardy. That Thomas's Welsh
inheritance was an important factor in the development
of his writing was early recognised by his Welsh critics.
Most of them have emphasised the significance of the fact
that he came from Swansea and not any other part of
Wales. Raymond Garlick, for example, in an essay on
Thomas published in 1954, after referring to "the distinc-
tive life of Swansea," says that "the Welshness of Dylan
Thomas cannot be too much stressed." He goes on to
quote from the tribute in the Welsh language broadcast
the day after Thomas's death by the distinguished poet
and critic, Saunders Lewis, who, as a Welsh-speaking
Welsh Nationalist, found that "Thomas brought honour
to Wales and in his later years he became more and more
Welsh in his sympathies. . . ."[1] Gwyn Jones, a Welsh-
speaking Professor of English, said: "Nor has Swansea
ever let him go."[2] The point has been emphasised more
recently by an English critic, Geoffrey Moore: "He went
back to South Wales because his heart was there and
because his themes of life and death and love were mostly
conceived in terms of the people, the places and the
institutions of South Wales."[3]

Thomas has given us his own vivid and unforgettable
picture of his early environment in his broadcast talks,
"Reminiscences of Childhood":

I was born in a large Welsh industrial town at the
beginning of the Great War: an ugly, lovely town (or
so it was, and is, to me), crawling, sprawling, slummed,
unplanned, jerry-villa'd, and smug-suburbed by the
side of a long and splendid-curving shore where truant

boys and sandfield boys and old anonymous men, in the tatters and hangovers of a hundred charity suits, beachcombed, idled, and paddled, watched the dock-bound boats, threw stones into the sea for the barking, outcast dogs, and, on Saturday summer afternoons, listened to the militant music of salvation and hell-fire preached from a soap-box.[4]

That Thomas's was not a particularly eccentric vision of his home and background can be witnessed by other writers. Professor Gwyn Jones, himself a Monmouth man and long domiciled in Cardigan, said in his eloquent testimonial to "Welsh Dylan":

If a poet must be born at all, this [*sc.* Swansea] is as good a place to choose as any, with its palmy welcome and humerus friendship, its wet-lip kiss and bosomy embrace. . . . Swansea . . . is a most diverting west Wales village of 150,000 people, with its notables and naturals, its musicians and poets and loose forwards, packed tight and lordly on the ground.[5]

This was the place where, on 22 Oct., 1914, the poet was born. He was named Dylan Marlais, and never has a child been given more apt and prophetic names. The second and less familiar of his given names means "voice of the sea"—it was an appropriate name for the poet who was to write:

> The bows glided down, and the coast
> Blackened with birds took a last look
> At his thrashing hair and whale-blue eye;
> The trodden town rang its cobbles for luck.[6]

and:

> The masses of the sea
> The masses of the sea under
> The masses of the infant-bearing sea
> Erupt, fountain, and enter to utter for ever

> Glory glory glory
> The sundering ultimate kingdom of genesis'
>   thunder.[7]

But it is his other given name by which he is deservedly known. As an Englishman who knew him well has said: "To a whole generation of writers—and to almost every Welshman of his time—he was simply 'Dylan'."[8] This magical and evocative name comes from the Fourth Branch of the Mabinogi, wherein the name is bestowed by the magician-king, Math son of Mathonwy on the son of Arianrhod (the Welsh White Goddess).

In the early nineteenth century the Welsh poet Islwyn wrote a poem called "Y Dylanwad," the title of which, according to H. Idris Bell, may be rendered as "Inspiration"; a poem which expressed the effect of romanticism on the centuries-old craft or sullen art of Welsh poets. According to Bell, "Y Dylanwad" is a poem which clearly expresses the conception of poetry as "a gift of the gods, the poet as an inspired seer, expressing his individual experiences, emotions and *Weltanschauung*." Islwyn, impatient of the highly complicated rules of Welsh bardism, says of poetry in words that recall Keats as well as many lesser Romantics:

> It comes when it will
>   Like the rainbow on the hill,
> Like the nightingale's song when the night is still;
> Not freer than it the spirits who play
> On the ebbing waves of the dying day,
> When the wide west seems, from the sun to the sea,
> But the flaming gate of Eternity.[9]

It is perhaps not the least of Dylan Thomas's achievements that he has managed to combine this sort of attitude with the nearest possible approach in the English language to the technical skill of the poets of the Welsh language—which, like many other Anglo-Welsh writers, he did not know. In an essay on these writers called "A Question of Language," Aneirin Talfan Davies denies that there are, as some critics unacquainted with Welsh poetry have asserted, direct formal influences from Welsh poetry to be found in Thomas's work, and he compares Thomas unfavourably in this respect with Gerard Manley Hopkins.[10] Aneirin Talfan is obviously right about the formal prosodic influence of Welsh poetry on that of Dylan Thomas; but in his justifiable eagerness to berate the ignorance of some English commentators, he himself misses the point about Thomas's use of language. No native English writer could so creatively have misused the English language in the peculiar fashion that charac-terises Thomas's poetry.

Dylan Thomas came, like almost every other Welshman of his generation, of country folk. His father was D. J. Thomas, Senior English Master at the Swansea Grammar School. The poet in later life wrote two poems about his father from which we can deduce without any other information that he loved and revered him. This inference is supported by other sources.

According to Suzanne Roussillat, whose biographical sketch is based on details given her by the poet himself, D. J. Thomas "was revered by his pupils for possessing the secret power of making them love and enjoy what he taught them"[11]—a not uncommon gift of Welshmen teaching English in Grammar Schools. Vernon Watkins says that D. J. Thomas "was an outstandingly good scholar and reader of Shakespeare. Father and son, who in modern literature liked different books, had a deep mutual respect and love."[12] The poet himself indirectly conveys the same impression in a letter he wrote to his parents on his first American tour:

After a reading in Indianapolis, a man came up to me and said, in a strong Swansea accent, "How's D.J. these days? He used to teach me English before the last war. I've been an American citizen now for 25 years." And he sounded as if he'd just stepped out from Morriston.[13]

The two poems speak eloquently for themselves:

> And you, my father, there on the sad height,
> Curse, bless, me now with your fierce tears, I pray.
> Do not go gentle into that good night.
> Rage, rage against the dying of the light.[14]

> Too proud to die, broken and blind he died
> The darkest way, and did not turn away,
> A cold kind man brave in his narrow pride.[15]

Thomas's childhood appears to have been a happy one. We might legitimately infer as much from stories like "The Fight" and poems like "Fern Hill" and "Poem in October"—"luminous with all the weathers of childhood," as Elder Olson describes them,[16] but there is plenty of other evidence as well, not least the testimony of his friends. Childhood, imaginatively happy childhood, is one of the constant themes of Thomas's prose and poetry; time and time again the adult writer recreates his own childhood joys in Cwmdonkin Park, in the Carmarthenshire countryside where he spent his holidays, and in his own home and that of his friend, Daniel Jones:

> While the boys among willows
> Made the tigers jump out of their eyes
> To roar on the rockery stones
> And the groves were blue with sailors[17]

> All the sun long it was running, it was lovely, the hay
> Fields high as the house, the tunes from the chimneys,
>   it was air
> And playing, lovely and watery
> And fire green as grass.[18]

Looking through my bedroom window, out into the moonlight and the flying, unending, smoke-coloured snow, I could see the lights in the windows of all the other houses on our hill, and hear the music rising from them up the long, steadily falling night. I turned the gas down, I got into bed. I said some words to the close and holy darkness, and then I slept.[19]

The room was splendidly untidy, full of wool and paper and open cupboards stacked with things you could never find; all the expensive furniture had been kicked; a waistcoat hung on the chandelier. I thought I could live for ever in that room, writing and fighting and spilling ink, having my friends for picnics there after midnight with Waller's rum-and-butter and Charlottes russes from Eynon's and Cydrax and Vino.[20]

Daniel Jones, the composer, whose room was the one described in this last extract, tells us that at the Grammar School Dylan Thomas was self-sufficient; though he took part in such usual school activities as contributing to and editing the school magazine, acting in school plays, debating with "a triumphant use of the illogical," he was resolutely unacademic, and his interest was obsessively in poetry. Daniel Jones is almost certainly right when he says that:

This early stand against the academic was very valu-able to Dylan; he would have needed twice the time to accomplish all that he did accomplish if he had not discerned clearly and from the beginning the things that were of no use to him, or if he had not steadily ignored them.[21]

It is important to remember also that Thomas grew up in an atmosphere of war and the threat of further war. Industrial ugliness and mass unemployment were familiar sights. His experience of these things, however, and his reaction to that experience, were very different from those of most of the English writers of that generation. In *New Writing in Europe*, John Lehmann tells us that the events and experiences of the nineteen-twenties and thirties were a traumatic shock to the young English writers of the time:

> It was in the years between 1929 and 1931 that a series of events took place that cracked the world of the 'twenties beyond repair. . . . People suddenly saw that Western society was not going to settle down to an era of ever-increasing riches and contentment. . . . Instead of increasing prosperity, the world was suddenly confronted with the paradox of poverty rampant at a time when more than enough had been and could be produced to meet the needs of all, of coffee and corn being wasted while hundreds of thousands went hungry. This was not really a new phenomenon, but it was new in its dimensions, and new to most of those in the prime of life in 1930. It was above all paralysing to all who had fed themselves with the illusion that such agonies were part and parcel of the bad old days which could never return.[22]

For Thomas there was nothing of this shocked reaction, and the reason lies in his heritage and his environment as well as in his individual temperament. Thomas was not at all what came to be known in the nineteen-thirties as a working-class writer: had he been English he would certainly have felt himself to be middle-class, and might even have had to wear a cloth cap as an emblem of rebellion against or emancipation from that state. In Wales, however, where traditionally intellect and learning are held in honour, the rigidities and asperities of the English class-system, if not altogether unknown, are blurred and softened. Thomas belonged to a community, not a class; and this in itself was enough to set him apart from the English "public-school" poets of the nineteen-thirties. To say this sort of thing is not to say that Thomas was ignorant of or indifferent to the ugly social reality of the world about him. In a broadcast talk on Welsh poets in 1946, he characterised the Rhymney poet, Idris Davies, as one of the poets out of the mining valleys of South Wales

who were beginning to write in a spirit of passionate anger against the inequalities of social conditions. They wrote, not of the truths and beauties of the natural world, but of the lies and ugliness of the unnatural system of society under which they worked—or, more often during the nineteen-twenties and thirties, under which they were not allowed to work. They spoke, in ragged and angry rhythms, of the Wales *they* knew: the coal-tips, the dole-queues, the stubborn bankrupt villages, the children, scrutting for coal on the slag-heaps, the colliers' shabby allotments, the cheapjack cinema, the whippet races, the disused quarries, the still pit-wheels, the gaunt tin-roofed chapels in the soot, the hewers squatting in the cut, the pubs, the Wool-worths, the deacons and the gyppos, silicosis, little Moscow beyond the hills, sag-roof factory and plume-less stack, stone-grey street, scummed river, the capped and mufflered knots of men outside the grim employ-ment exchange and the public library.[23]

The difference between Thomas and such class-conscious English poets as Auden, Day Lewis, and Spender were in the nineteen-thirties is that he did not take all this as involving any personal guilt—it was, like the hunchback in Cwmdonkin Park and the "old girls in the snug" and the view of the bay (which Landor, as the locals have not forgotten, once compared to the Bay of Naples)—it was all, for the young Thomas, simply and excitingly part of "the world I breathe." In a sense it is true, as Elder Olson has said, that in an age when poetry was expected to have social reference, an age when even *The Waste Land* was valued as a social document, the

B

poems of Dylan Thomas had no social reference. If we look closely at the early poems, however, we can find in them some evidence for Thomas's awareness of social reality. (There is more in the stories of the *Portrait*.) The famous "boys of summer in their ruin," for example, apart from their symbolic significance, are particularly the young "voters" or "elements" who haunt the stories of Gwyn Thomas. And while many indignant poems of the decade now moulder away with other forgotten propaganda, the genuine compassion of "Paper and Sticks" (the words of which are obviously spoken by Lily Smalls) is as moving as when it was first written:

> Paper and sticks and shovel and match
> Why won't the news of the old world catch
> And the fire in a temper start
>
> Sharp and shrill my silly tongue scratches
> Words on the air as the fire catches
> *You* never did and *he* never did.[24]

I have already referred to Thomas's self-sufficiency as a grammar-school boy; his resistance to the academic and to all that did not directly concern him, and his determined obsession with poetry. He has himself told us as much in one of the stories of the *Portrait* which sharply and amusingly records the beginning of his lifelong friendship with the Swansea composer, Daniel Jones. The story begins, as their acquaintance did, with a fight. Thomas goes on to describe himself walking to his new friend's house for the first time, and reciting to himself as he went pieces of his own poems. The story ends:

At the corner, Dan said: 'I must leave you now, I've got to finish a string trio tonight.'

'I'm working on a long poem,' I said, 'about the princes of Wales and the wizards and everybody.'

We both went home to bed.[25]

That in this story Thomas is not exaggerating his schoolboy preoccupation is impressively shown in the files of the *Swansea Grammar School Magazine*. In his last year at school he also began to contribute articles to a local newspaper, the *Herald of Wales*, on such subjects as "The Poets of Swansea, Walter Savage Landor to James Chapman Woods," "Tragedy of Swansea's Comic Genius. The story of Llewelyn Prichard, Author of Twm Shon Catti," and "Minor Poets of Old Swansea...." Given his attitude and his obsession, and with such a record behind him, it was not at all surprising that Thomas, whose father had wished him to work for a university scholarship, should on leaving school begin work for a local newspaper. This was the *South Wales Evening Post*, on which he worked as a reporter for a year (1931–2). On this brief but important period of his life the best evidence is again his own writings—we have the testimony of friends, notably Daniel Jones, to their general authenticity.

There is, for example, the little sketch of Thomas the young reporter in "Return Journey," that memorable work for radio which is itself, among other things, a very good job of reporting.

First Young Reporter: What you been reporting today, Young Thomas?

Second Young Reporter: Two typewriter Thomas the ace news-dick. . . .

Old Reporter: Let's have a dekko at your note-book. Called at British Legion: Nothing. Called at Hospital: One broken leg. Auction at the Metropole. Ring Mr. Beynon *re* Gymanfa Ganu. Lunch: Pint and pasty at the Singleton with Mrs. Giles. Bazaar at Bethesda Chapel. Chimney on fire at Tontine Street. Walters Road Sunday School Outing. Rehearsal of the *Mikado* at Skewen—all front page stuff.[26]

This "Young Thomas" is recognisably the same person as the young reporter of "Old Garbo," sharing in the office lavatory of the *Tawe News*

> a great male moment . . . a small wickedness with an old, important man. I should have been writing up last night's performance of *The Crucifixion* or loitering, with my new hat on one side, through the Christmas-Satur-day-crowded town in the hopes of an accident. . . .[27]

It is all too easy to treat certain aspects of, certain incidents in, an artist's life and career in a dramatic or even melodramatic manner. The writer-about-Dylan-Thomas (and particularly one from a similar background) is tempted to say that the first fatal step which he took towards that premature death in New York was the one that put him, following the example of many other young men from the provinces and the Principality, on a train for London. We need not take too seriously the account he gives in *Adventures* of his departure from Swansea and his arrival in the metropolis. As in the *Portrait*, biographical elements are obviously involved here. It is equally obvious that in the later work exaggeration and caricature are used more deliberately. Exaggeration and caricature had been present in the stories of the *Portrait*, but in *Adventures* they become dominant modes:

> Dear mother, he wrote with his finger on the back of an envelope, looking up, between every few invisible words, at the unnoticing woman opposite, this is to tell you that I arrived safely and that I am drinking in the buffet with a tart. . . .[28]

Anyway, there the young Welsh poet was in London, looking like a cherub and bound to be painted by Augustus John (whom he first met in the Fitzroy Tavern, and who was to be later responsible for introducing him to Caitlin Macnamara who became his wife). Thomas, who at first shared a flat with two painters, Mervyn Levy, and his own old Swansea friend, Alfred Janes, rapidly made many acquaintances and friends in London. Most of these were connected with literature and the arts in one way or another.

More important, he began to have his poems published in magazines where they were noticed. R. N. Maud has discovered that his first actual English publication was an early version of "And Death shall have no Dominion," in *The New English Weekly*, IV (18 May 1933).[29] But the one that really mattered was the prize-winning poem in Victor Neuberg's poetry column in *The Sunday Referee* on 3 Sep. 1933. Thomas never reprinted this poem, "That Sanity be Kept," but in the next twelve months his prize-winning poems in the same column included "The Force that through the Green Fuse Drives the Flower," "A Process in the Weather of the Heart," and "Where once the Waters of your Face." In the same year he published poems in *The Adelphi*, *The Listener*, *New Verse*, and the *Criterion*. The achievement was an astonishing one for a young and unknown poet, and it led rapidly to the publication of his first volume, *18 Poems*, little more than a year after his arrival in London. Thomas himself was later to refer humorously to the achievement as an example of "The Provincial Rush, or the Up-Rimbaud-and-At-'Em approach" which, for success, required behind it "a body (it need have no head) of ferocious and un-understandable verse."[30] The achievement remains.

A statement often made, in some form or other, about these early poems by Thomas is that they are obsessively about three things, and three things only: birth, copulation, and death. That Thomas's early poems, or most of them, are about birth, copulation, and death is true enough in a way; but to say so is by no means to say the whole truth about these extraordinary, fascinating, and often baffling poems.

Indeed, one of the most straightforward, readily intelligible, and best, of the early poems "Especially when the

October Wind," can scarcely be said to be about these "facts" at all. The poem is about two things which become one thing in the very act of writing about them: the natural scene, "the loud hill of Wales," and the writing of poetry inspired by that scene:

> Some let me make you of the vowelled beeches,
> Some of the oaken voices, from the roots
> Of many a thorny shire tell you notes,
> Some let me make you of the water's speeches.[31]

Thomas himself has been pretty ribald at the expense of "nature poets." His Civil Service poet writes a poem:

It is, of course, about Nature; it confesses a wish to escape from humdrum routine and embrace the unsophisticated life of the farm labourer; he desires, though without scandal, to wake up with the birds; he expresses the opinion that a ploughshare, not a pen, best fits his little strength; a decorous pantheist, he is one with the rill, the rhyming mill, the rosy-bottomed milkmaid, the russet-cheeked rat-catcher, swains, swine, pipits, pippins. You can smell the country in his poems, the fields, the flowers, the armpits of Triptolemus, the barns, the pyres, the hay, and, most of all, the corn.[32]

Despite this, Thomas was a nature poet in the sense that much of his truest inspiration arose from a natural scene which he had contemplated long and lovingly. This is particularly to be seen in poems like "Prologue," "Over Sir John's Hill," and "Poem on his Birthday."[33]

Certainly, Thomas's obsession with birth, copulation, and death is present and prominent in the early poems— no reader could well deny that. And certainly, too, our dominant impression as we read is that Thomas is obsessed by these. One is tempted to say that these poems are about what another Welsh poet, Alun Lewis, called "the single poetic theme of life and death."[34]

Some typical lines indicate clearly enough where the difference lies:

> I see the summer children in their mothers
> Split up the brawned womb's weathers.
>
> I smelt the maggot in my stool.
>
> And I am dumb to tell the lover's tomb
> How at my sheet goes the same crooked worm.[35]

At first, this does look like the poetry approvingly or disapprovingly described by various critics as poetry of the elemental physical experience. Closer attention reveals that, although Thomas is indeed talking about this, he is doing so in an individual way. A poem which most clearly illustrates this is "Light Breaks where no Sun Shines:"

> Light breaks where no sun shines;
> Where no sea runs, the waters of the heart
> Push in their tides;
> And, broken ghosts with glow-worms in their heads,
> The things of light
> File through the flesh where no flesh decks the bones.
>
> A candle in the thighs
> Warms youth and seed and burns the seeds of age;
> Where no seed stirs,
> The fruit of man unwrinkles in the stars,
> Bright as a fig;
> Where no wax is, the candle shows its hairs.
>
> Dawn breaks behind the eyes;
> From poles of skull and toe the windy blood
> Slides like a sea;
> Nor fenced, nor staked, the gushers of the sky
> Spout to the rod
> Divining in a smile the oil of tears.

Night in the sockets rounds,
Like some pitch moon, the limit of the globes;
Day lights the bone;
Where no cold is, the skinning gales unpin
The winter's robes;
The film of spring is hanging from the lids.

Light breaks on secret lots,
On tips of thought where thoughts smell in the rain;
When logics die,
The secret of the soil grows through the eye,
And blood jumps in the sun;
Above the waste allotments the dawn halts.[36]

This is one of the best-organised of Thomas's early poems. It is written in a regular stanza and in predominantly iambic metre (the variations consisting of extra stresses and inversions). Thomas uses the devices of rhyme, assonance, near-rhyme, alliteration, repetition, and what may be called associative repetition ("light, sun, dawn," "sea, waters, tides") to construct an elaborately formal poem. All the devices point to the fact that the poem consists of a repetitive series of statements, of which the first is the most important. The sexual imagery of the poem makes it clear that "where no sun shines . . . Where no seed stirs . . . Where no wax is . . . Where no cold is . . ." is in man's existence at the moment of conception. The poem is about the embryo; and since, etymologically, the word implies the idea "to contain, to be full of," its subsequent development, in writing of the embryo Thomas also writes of all that will happen to it, particularly old age and death. The theme of the poem might be summed up as the simple statement that life is a process, something that goes on and that death is implicit from the very moment of conception.

The poem "If I were Tickled by the Rub of Love"[37] is obviously one of those which have something, at least, to do with birth, copulation, and death. The three most striking things that the attentive reader notices about the poem, however, are the regular seven-lined stanzas, the repetition of the words "rub" and "tickled," and the fact that the total structure of the poem depends mainly on these two repetitions, one formal, one verbal. The poem is in three parts. The first four stanzas are each built around the "If I were tickled . . . I would not fear . . ." construction (with a slight variation in st. 4). Sts. 5 and 6 make a series of positive statements about the poet's, or rather the speaker's, own situation; the central statement, "And that's the rub, the only rub that tickles," referring back to the first part. The last stanza asks, "And what's the rub?", supplies three possible answers and, in the last two lines, a conclusion:

> I would be tickled by the rub that is:
> Man be my metaphor.

We take the word "rub" at first in its sexual connotation, but its repetition reminds us of its old meaning of obstacle, impediment; of Hamlet who said, "Ay, there's the rub," and of Richard II's Queen for whom "the world is full of rubs." *Hamlet*, we also remember, is a play much obsessed with sex, disease, and death, as the speaker in this poem is, particularly in the first four stanzas. There, he says that under certain conditions he would not fear certain things: if he were an unborn child again, he would not fear sin, punishment, or the miseries of adolescence; if he were a child again, he would not fear violent death; if he were an adolescent again, he would fear neither sex nor death; if he were sufficiently "tickled by," absorbed in, the act of sex, "the lovers' rub," he would not fear the degeneration of age. The implication is that since these conditions do not obtain, he does fear these things, and suffer from them. This implication is borne out, as Olson noticed,[38] by the language and imagery employed:

If I were tickled by the lovers' rub
That wipes away not crow's foot nor the lock
Of sick old manhood on the fallen jaws,
Time and the crabs and the sweethearting crib
Would leave me cold as butter for the flies,
The sea of scums could drown me as it broke
Dead on the sweethearts' toes.

What has been implicit is made explicit in st. 5, where
we learn that the speaker is in love, but shares the world
with the Devil, is already one with the old man he must
become, and, again like Hamlet, is terribly aware of
all this. It is indeed in the very contemplation of his
condition—

I sit and watch the worm beneath my nail
Wearing the quick away

that he finds the real justification of life, "the only rub
that tickles." St. 6 rejects the condition of unawareness,
of being the mere "knobbly ape that swings along the
sex." In the last stanza he asks himself what is this "only
rub that tickles"? To this question he gives three possible
answers: death itself, sexual love, the Christian religion;
and he concludes that all he knows is that this is the
human condition.

Only after analysing the poem in this way are we justified in tentatively identifying the "I" of the poem with the
poet himself. The main body of the poem is about the
"wearisome condition of humanity"; and it is not so
much, as Marshall W. Stearns suggested,[39] that Thomas
here "selects *man* as the theme of his poetry" as that in the
poem itself he makes it evident that man is his theme.
"Man be my metaphor": Thomas said it early, and he
was still saying it in later life, briefly in the Note to
Collected Poems, at more length in his broadcast statement
about the projected long poem "In Country Sleep."[40]

At the time when he was writing the poems collected

in his first volume, Thomas wrote a poem called "Jack of Christ." He never published this poem, and phrases from it (including the title, which occurs in the last stanza of the poem just examined) crop up in various other poems of the time. In 1934 he gave a typescript of the poem to the Welsh writer, Glyn Jones, who allowed it to be published in the *Western Mail* in 1960.[41] The poem, which is in three parts, consists of 113 lines. Though not in itself one of Thomas's best poems, it is one that is both technically and thematically very important to the understanding of Thomas, since it reveals very clearly that consistency of all his poetry on which W. S. Merwin has remarked.[42] In particular, in this very early poem we find Thomas overtly displaying his essentially religious nature and that "love of man" he claimed in the note to *Collected Poems*:

> Where is no God there man believes,
> And where God is his homage turns to dust;
> God who is all tells in His desert gust
> That one man must
> Be all and all be one. . . .

Such a poem is more revealing of the direction Thomas's early work was taking than are the replies he made to a *New Verse* questionnaire in 1934. Here, Thomas made the statement that he had been influenced by Freud (which is by no means the same thing as saying he had read Freud):

> Freud cast light on a little of the darkness he had exposed. Benefiting by the sight of the light and the knowledge of the hidden nakedness, poetry must drag further into the clean nakedness of light more even of the hidden causes than Freud could realise.[43]

The most interesting aspect of Thomas's replies to this rather inept questionnaire is that here he does what he did later in a letter to Henry Treece[44] about his method of writing poems. In both cases, Thomas goes to some length to explain carefully what he feels to be his procedure: in both cases, his explanations are a little less than convincing.

This statement about the influence of Freud has been often quoted by Thomas's critics. Much more revealing of the true nature of his poetry are his answers to the first and last of the six questions posed by Geoffrey Grigson, the editor of *New Verse*. In answer to the first question: "Do you intend your poetry to be useful to yourself or others?" Thomas said:

> To both ... My poetry is, or should be, useful to me for one reason: it is the record of my individual struggle from darkness towards some measure of light ... My poetry is, or should be, useful to others for its individual recording of that same struggle. ...

And to the question, "As a poet what distinguishes you, do you think, from an ordinary man?" Thomas replied:

> Only the use of the medium of poetry to express the causes and forces which are the same in all men.

Here, in all sincerity, speaks the poet who saw "the boys of summer in their ruin," who

> was brother to Mnetha's daughter
> And sister to the fathering worm,

who "would be tickled by the rub that is:" the poet for whom "Man be my metaphor" had been a fulfilled wish since he had begun to write; the poet who would say truthfully, years later, in the Note prefixed to his *Collected Poems*:

> These poems, with all their crudities, doubts and confusions, are written for the love of Man and in praise of God, and I'd be a damn' fool if they weren't.[45]

It is all in the poem "Jack of Christ."

REFERENCES

1. Raymond Garlick, "The Endless Breviary," in *The Month*, ii (1954), 144.

2. Gwyn Jones, "Welsh Dylan," in *The Adelphi*, xxx (1954), 111.

3. Geoffrey Moore, "Dylan Thomas," in *Dylan Thomas: The Legend and the Poet*, ed. E. W. Tedlock (henceforth cited as Tedlock), London 1960, p. 253.

4. "Reminiscences of Childhood" (First Version), in *Q.E.O.M.*, p. 1.

5. Gwyn Jones, "Welsh Dylan," in *The Adelphi*, xxx (1954), 111.

6. "Ballad of the Long-legged Bait," in *C.P.*, p. 149.

7. "Ceremony after a Fire Raid," in *C.P.*, p. 131.

8. John Arlott, "Dylan Thomas and Radio," in *The Adelphi*, xxx (1954), 121.

9. H. Idris Bell, *The Nature of Poetry as conceived by the Welsh Bards*, Oxford 1955, p. 4.

10. Aneirin Talfan Davies, "A Question of Language," in *Yr Einion*, v (1953), 26.

11. Suzanne Roussillat, in *Adam International Review*, 238 (1953), 66.

12. Vernon Watkins, in a letter to the author.

13. Printed in J. M. Brinnin, *Dylan Thomas in America*, London 1956, p. 56.

14. "Do not go Gentle ...," in *C.P.*, p. 116.

15. *New Poems, 1956*, edd. Stephen Spender and others, London 1956, pp. 60–1.

16. Elder Olson, "The Poetry of Dylan Thomas," in Tedlock, p. 231.

17. "The Hunchback in the Park," in *C.P.*, p. 112.

18. "Fern Hill," in *C.P.*, p. 159.

19. "Conversation about Christmas," in *Prospect*, p. 103.

20. "The Fight," in *Portrait*, pp. 81–2.

21. Daniel Jones, in Tedlock, pp. 17, 18.

22. John Lehmann, *New Writing in Europe*, London 1940, pp. 19–20.

23. "Welsh Poets," in *Q.E.O.M.*, pp. 147–8.

24. "Paper and Sticks," in *D.E.*, p. 23.

25. "The Fight," in *Portrait*, pp. 94–5.

26. *Q.E.O.M.*, pp. 79–80.

27. *Portrait*, pp. 185–6.

28. *Adventures*, p. 38.

29. R. N. Maud, "Dylan Thomas's first Published Poem," in *M.L.N.*, lxxiv (1959), 117.

30. "How to be a Poet," in *Prospect*, p. 114.

31. "Especially when the October Wind," in *C.P.*, pp. 16–17.

32. "How to be a Poet," in *Prospect*, pp. 105–6.

33. In *C.P.*, pp. vii, 167, 170.

34. Alun Lewis, *Ha! Ha! Among the Trumpets*, London 1945, p. 12.

35. *C.P.*, pp. 1, 8, 9.
36. "Light Breaks . . . ," in *C.P.*, p. 24.
37. In *C.P.*, pp. 12–13.
38. Olson, *The Poetry of Dylan Thomas*, pp. 37–40.
39. Marshall Stearns, "Unsex the Skeleton," in Tedlock, p. 116.
40. "Three Poems," in *Q.E.O.M.*, pp. 155–67.
41. Glyn Jones, in a letter to the author. *Western Mail*, 30 July, 1960.
42. W. S. Merwin, "The Religious Poet," in *Adam International Review*, 238 (1953), 73.
43. *New Verse*, XI (1934), 8–9.
44. Henry Treece, *Dylan Thomas*, London 1949, pp. 47–8.
45. *C.P.*, p. vi.

CHAPTER II

THE MAP OF LOVE

These early years spent mainly in London appear to have been happy and busy ones for Thomas. He had many friends, including Vernon Watkins, whom he had met soon after the publication of *18 Poems*; he was already famous; he was making some sort of a living from his poems and from reviewing. During the early years in London he was writing, and publishing, short stories as well as poems. Perhaps "short stories" is not the right name for the prose pieces eventually collected in *The Map of Love*—H. G. Porteous once suggested that they be called "lyrical fables,"[1] and the term is in many respects apt. Certainly the difference between these and the later stories collected as *Portrait of the Artist as a Young Dog* (the title was suggested by Richard Hughes)[2] is greater than that between the early poems and those that Thomas wrote after the beginning of the War; though, as I shall show later, both his prose and his poetry underwent similar developments.

Thomas's prose is admittedly inferior to his poetry, but it is part of his total creative output, and it is not without interest and importance of its own. Vernon Watkins refers aptly to "the struggling, symbol-charged prose of the intensely subjective early stories."[3] Here, for example, is a passage from "The Mouse and the Woman":

Consider now the old effigies of the seasons. Break up the rhythm of the old figures' moving, the spring trot, summer canter, sad stride of autumn, and winter shuffle. Break, piece by piece, the continuous changing

of motion into a spindle-shanked walking. Consider the
sun for whom I know no image but the old image of a
shot eye, and the broken moon.[4]

And here are the last two sentences of "In the Direction
of the Beginning":

He marked her outcast image, mapped with a night-
mare's foot in poison and framed against the wind,
print of her thumb that buckled on its hand with a
webbed shadow, interrogation of the familiar echo:
which is my genesis, the granite fountain extinguishing
where the first flame is cast in the sculptured world, or
the bonfire maned like a lion in the threshold of the last
vault? One voice then in that evening travelled the
light and water waves, one lineament took on two
sliding moods, from where the gold green sea cantharis
dyes the trail of the octopus one venom crawled
through foam, and from the four map corners one
cherub in an island shape puffed the clouds to sea.[5]

Such passages show that what Thomas is trying to do
in these prose pieces is, as Aneirin Talfan Davies suggested of all Anglo-Welsh writers, nothing much more
than to emulate his own idiot in "The Tree":

Bethlehem, said the idiot to the valley, turning over the
sounds of the word and giving it all the glory of the
Welsh morning.[6]

It is obviously tempting to say that these early stories are
typical products of a young poet trying, without too
much understanding of its true nature, "the other harmony of prose." And that they are more like poems in
prose than what we normally understand by the term
"short stories" is even more obviously true. The prose,
even in the more explicitly narrative passages, is always
self-consciously poetic:

He walked to the last rail before pitch space; though the earth bowled round quickly, he saw every plough crease and beast's print, man track and water drop, comb, crest, and plume mark, dust and death groove and signature and time-cast shade, from icefield to icefield, sea rims to sea centres, all over the apple-shaped ball under the metal rails beyond the living doors.[7]

But these "lyrical fables" are not merely poems in prose or surrealistic attempts to give English words "all the glory of the Welsh morning." The seven stories which Thomas collected in *The Map of Love* (together with the first three stories in *Prospect* and uncollected ones like "The Burning Baby" and "The School for Witches"[8]) have a common topography: they are all set in the country of "the Jarvis Hills," that is, in the Carmarthenshire countryside which was later to provide the background for such stories as "A Visit to Grandpa's"[9] and for so many of Thomas's best poems. This common topography, although never very clearly defined, does reinforce the common atmosphere of the stories; and they do, in fact, gain from being read as some sort of a loosely-connected series rather than as separate pieces. But even read as separate stories, odd though they often seem, they *are* stories, in the sense that they do have characters and plots or themes, however slight these may be or however difficult to find in the luxuriant jungle of the prose. In "A Prospect of the Sea,"[10] a small dreaming boy meets a girl, and loses her; in "After the Fair"[11] a runaway girl meets the Fat Man at the fair, and rides with him on the roundabouts to keep a baby from crying; in "The Visitor,"[12] a poet dies; in "The Map of Love,"[13] a boy and girl initiate each other into sex. The most powerful, and in some ways perhaps the best, of these stories is "The Enemies."[14] In this story an old clergyman, Mr Davies, is lost in the morning on the Jarvis hills. In a lonely valley he comes upon the house of a young

c

couple, Mr and Mrs Owen. They have, we are told, deliberately chosen this valley to live in because of its loneliness. Mrs Owen is a crystal-gazer, who has been watching the old man as he stumbles about the hills. The couple take Mr Davies in for a rest and a meal. They are kind to him, but there is something sinister in their kindness: when he says grace before the meal, "he could not hear what they said, but he knew the prayers they spoke were not his prayers." Then Mr Davies tells them "in a sweet delirium" of his misadventures that morning:

> "He is frightened of the dark," thought Mrs. Owen, "the lovely dark." With a smile, Mr. Owen thought: "He is frightened of the worm in the earth, of the copulation in the tree, of the living grease in the soil."

The story ends with the old clergyman suddenly kneeling down to pray:

> Kneeling on the carpet at the head of the table, he stared in bewilderment at the dark mind and the gross dark body. He stared and he prayed, like an old god beset by his enemies.

This story of an encounter with ancient, pagan, "dark" forces is told with admirable economy and clarity, as is the simple and moving story of the madman, "The Dress".[15]

All these stories share certain other features in common. Apart from the unnamed woman in "The Dress" there are no normal characters in the stories. The main characters are children, madmen, and poets. Because of this, there is in most of them an effect of blurring the boundaries between reality and fantasy, between fact and dream. Did Mr Davies really get lost like that on the Jarvis hills? Or did it all happen in his mind? What really happened to the boy in "A Prospect of the Sea," or the children in "The Map of Love," or the boy Marlais in "The Orchards"? Did the boy in "The Trees" really crucify the Idiot? To ask the questions thus naïvely is to see how irrelevant they are. The informing theme of the whole series is, that for children, madmen, and poets, the normal, adult distinction between reality and fantasy, fact and dream, does not exist. It is a mark of Thomas's imagination that he can thus convince us, as we read, that we are inside the mind of a child or a madman.

It is always, of course, the mind of a poet. We have already noticed that the prose of these stories is always self-consciously poetic. But we should also notice how Thomas combines imagination and "poetic" writing with an extremely vivid attention to close detail. Consider, for example, the description of the pencil with which Marlais is trying to write a poem:

He raised his pencil so that its shadow fell, a tower of wood and lead, on the clean paper; he fingered the pencil tower, the half-moon of his thumb-nail rising and setting behind the leaden spire.[16]

Finally, we should notice that all these stories (except "The Lemon" and perhaps "The Burning Baby") possess a quality which was to become more and more marked in Thomas's later poetry and in his later prose—the quality of compassion. Annie, the runaway girl afraid of policemen; Peter, the dying poet; the frightened and bewildered old clergyman; the escaped madman who wants only to sleep—all these personages are treated with the same sympathetic understanding as the dreaming boy with the poet's own name, Marlais. Thomas's attitude is indeed expressed with beautiful concision by the madman in "The Dress":

Pity the hare, he thought, for the weasel will drink her.[17]

Terrible and fantastic things may happen in these stories, but Thomas writes of them out of pity and a will to understand, not out of wilfulness or a diseased imagination.

Thomas's second volume of poems was *Twenty-five Poems* in 1936. Most critics of Thomas's poetry have discussed his first two volumes together; and it is true that these two volumes have much in common, and may in some respects be treated as an entity. But certain differences can be detected, too. Some of Thomas's earlier critics, notably Henry Treece and Francis Scarfe, complained of a tendency to rhythmical monotony in the poems of his first two volumes. Most of his lines are end-stopped or virtually so, and when this is combined, as it usually is, with a predominantly iambic beat, the poems may be read insensitively so as to produce an effect of hammering repetitiveness. Once, in introducing a reading, Thomas himself referred to these early poems as having "vehement beat-pounding black and green rhythms like those of a very young policeman exploding."[18] On the other hand, Thomas displays great technical skill in the avoidance of rhythmical monotony under these circumstances by the use of reversed feet, feminine endings, and what R. N. Maud has called the breaking of the line "in a manner appropriate to the rhetorical flow of the verse,"[19] and punctuating it accordingly:

> The force that through the green fuse drives the flower
> Drives my green age; that blasts the roots of trees
> Is my destroyer.
> And I am dumb to tell the crooked rose
> My growth is bent by the same wintry fever.[20]

The too-regular rhythmical beat, hovering on the edge of monotony, is however undoubtedly present in the early poems, and in some of them it goes over the edge and becomes monotony:

> Before I knocked and flesh let enter,
> With liquid hands tapped on the womb,
> I who was shapeless as the water

> That shaped the Jordan near my home
> Was brother to Mnetha's daughter
> And sister to the fathering worm.[21]

—the pattern varies only minutely in the succeeding stanzas. This tendency is all the more surprising when we consider the rhythmical subtlety of which Thomas had already shown himself capable in some of the poems of his boyhood:

> Here is the bright green sea
> And underneath a thousand fishes
> Moving their scaly bodies soundlessly
> Among a bright green world of weeds.
> These thousand pebbles are a thousand eyes,
> Each sharper than the sun;
> These waves are dancers;
> Upon a thousand, pointed toes
> They step the sea,
> Lightly, as in a pantomime.[22]

Moreover, as one of his B.B.C. producers said in his memorial essay:

> He read with care for rhythm, and with a subtle gift for indicating a line-end when the meaning ran on un-punctuated without destroying the flow by a pause.[23]

In *Twenty-five Poems* we see Thomas making an effort to avoid the tyranny of the end-stopped iambic penta-meter. This could account for his inclusion in the volume, against the advice of Vernon Watkins, of the two poems "Now, Say Nay," and "How soon the Servant Sun," which are rhythmically subtle and interesting but as Watkins justly observes, present "a face of unwarrantable obscurity":

> Now
> Say nay,

No say sir
Yea the dead stir,
And this, nor this, is shade, the landed crow,
He lying low with ruin in his ear,
The cockerel's tide upcasting from the fire.[24]

Where Thomas's second volume really differs from his
first is in the inclusion of poems which both escape the
dominance of the end-stopped iambic line, whether of
three, four, or five beats, and present the reader with a
readily intelligible meaning:

> Ears in the turrets hear
> Hands grumble on the door,
> Eyes in the gables see
> The fingers at the locks.
> Shall I unbolt or stay
> Alone till the day I die
> Unseen by stranger-eyes
> In this white house?
> Hands, hold you poison or grapes?[25]

> The five kings count the dead but do not soften
> The crusted wound nor stroke the brow;
> A hand rules pity as a hand rules heaven;
> Hands have no tears to flow.[26]

> I have longed to move away
> From the repetition of salutes,
> For there are ghosts in the air
> And ghostly echoes on paper,
> And the thunder of calls and notes.[27]

As these extracts also show, there is in *Twenty-five
Poems* an extension of Thomas's scope—even less than in
18 Poems is he here merely the poet of "birth, copulation,
and death," except in so far as these themes are scarcely
avoidable in poetry. The poems range from the subjec-

tivity of "I, in my Intricate Image," to the objectivity of "The Hand that Signed a Paper." And the most important, though not necessarily the most successful, poem in the volume, the sonnet sequence "Altarwise by Owl-Light" reveals overtly for the first time that Thomas's main concern is a religious one.

Several critics, including Francis Scarfe and Marshall W. Stearns, have attempted to elucidate this fascinating, apparently baffling, and sometimes irritating, poem. Scarfe, for example, says that the poem represents "a double pattern of Biblical and sexual imagery."[28] This is true enough, but the only interpretation that makes complete sense of the poem is that propounded by Elder Olson in the only serious book-length study of Thomas's poetry that has so far appeared. Recognising that the main source of the poem's difficulty lies in its symbolism, Olson finds that that symbolism involves at least six distinguishable and intricately inter-related levels:

(1) A level based on the analogy of human life to the span of a year, which permits the use of phenomena of the seasons to represent events of human life, and vice versa;

(2) A level based on an analogy between the sun and man, permitting the attributes of each to stand for those of the other;

(3) A level of Thomas's "private" symbolism;

(4) A level based on ancient myth, principally Greek, representing the fortunes of the sun in terms of the adventures of the sun-hero Hercules;

(5) A level based on relations of the *constellation* Hercules to other constellations and astronomical phenomena; and

(6) A level derived from the Christian interpretation of levels (4) and (5).[29]

In the note at the beginning of the book Thomas stated that the ten sonnets were part of a work in progress.

Earlier, when the first seven were published in *Life and
Letters Today*, he had told the editors, "It's the first
passage of what's going to be a very long poem indeed."[30]
As far as is known, no more of this "very long poem" was
ever written. There are two possible explanations for this:
either the density and intricacy of the ten sonnets were
too much for even Thomas's ingenuity and technical
skill to continue; or, more probably, he came to feel that
the poem is in fact complete as it stands, beginning as it
does with the poet's intense and bitter realisation of
mortality and death:

> Altarwise by owl-light in the half-way house
> The gentleman lay graveward with his furies;[31]

and concluding with his hope and confidence in the day
of Resurrection:

> Green as beginning, let the garden diving
> Soar, with its two bark towers, to that Day
> When the worm builds with the gold straws of venom
> My nest of mercies in the rude, red tree.[32]

In 1937, the year after the publication of *Twenty-five
Poems*, Dylan Thomas associated himself somewhat more
closely with the elemental processes that had been playing such a large part in his poetry and prose by getting
married. (Rolph's bibliography antedates the event by
one year.) The late Augustus John has given us a charm-
ing account of how the poet met his wife. Caitlin
Macnamara, the daughter of an old friend of John's, was
staying with the painter as the guest of Richard Hughes
in Laugharne, near Carmarthen. John used to drive her
around the countryside. "One day we picked up Dylan
somewhere. It was easy to see that these two instantly fell
for each other. There was no mistake about it and I
wasn't surprised."[33] (Augustus John's memory seems to
have been slightly at fault; in a revised version of this

essay he alters the story somewhat. And Richard Hughes says that the couple actually met for the first time in his house, Laugharne Castle, John having invited Dylan there.)[34] In the letter to Vernon Watkins announcing his marriage, Thomas confirms John's impression (which is also that of Richard Hughes): "We've been meaning to from the first day we met, and now we are free and glad."[35]

After her husband's death, Caitlin Thomas created an unfortunate impression in the minds of many people, and, as the poet himself might have said, set a very libidinous cat loose among the presbyterian pigeons, with the publication of her unhappy and in some respects misguided book, *Leftover Life to Kill*. It is, one supposes, one of the accretions of the "Dylan Legend," and the critic of the poetry might, or ought, to be content to let it lie. The book, however, has a biographical importance as far as the poet himself is concerned. Too many people are only too eager to believe the worst of poets, as well apparently as of their wives. Thomas's marriage was one of the most fundamentally important things that ever happened to him, and any biographical account, however brief, must try to assess—and humanely—the true nature of that marriage.

To the reasonably unprejudiced reader who is not hot-foot in pursuit of scandal, a chief impression, and a deeply moving one, left by the pyrotechnical prose of Caitlin Thomas's book, is that she and Dylan were, and remained, deeply and genuinely in love. To say this is not to claim that they were ever potential claimants for the Dunmow Flitch. Reading John Malcolm Brinnin's unavoidably selective and obviously bewildered account of Caitlin and Dylan, one is often enough reminded of Frieda and D. H. Lawrence.

The evidence of *Leftover Life to Kill* supports the accounts given by Augustus John and Roy Campbell, both of whom knew the Thomases well, of their love for each other and happiness together. Even Brinnin, who first met Thomas in America in 1950, says: "I came early to understand that Dylan loved his wife with a singleness of passion and a serenity of heart which his other passions could never confuse."[36] In the first years of their marriage the Thomases lived in various places, first in Cornwall, then at Caitlin's home in Hampshire, and finally in Laugharne, "a fishing-village at the end of the world," as Vernon Watkins calls it. Their first child, Llewelyn, was born in 1939.

In his early married years, Thomas continued writing both prose and poetry at a fairly steady rate. Vernon Watkins finds a definite and significant change in Thomas's work about this time. The change, he says, is first apparent in a short poem about Cwmdonkin Park which Thomas sent to him on 29 Dec. 1938. "Both in poetry and prose his work from this time forward moved in the direction of the living voice."[37] This was the poem:

Once it was the colour of saying
Soaked my table the uglier side of a hill
With a capsized field where a school sat still
And a black and white patch of girls grew playing;
The gentle seaslides of saying I must undo
That all the charmingly drowned arise to cockcrow
    and kill.
When I whistled with mitching boys through a reser-
    voir park
Where at night we stoned the cold and cuckoo
Lovers in the dirt of their leafy beds,
The shade of their trees was a word of many shades
And a lamp of lightning for the poor in the dark;
Now my saying shall be my undoing,
And every stone I wind off like a reel.[38]

This is a poem that anticipates in many ways most of the poems Thomas was to write from now on. In it, there is the evocation of childhood that was to find its most

lyrical expression in "Poem in October" and "Fern Hill";
there is the association of the natural scene with love-
making

> the close and cuckoo
> Lovers in the dirt of their leafy beds . . .

with which compare:

> And there this night I walk in the white giant's thigh
> Where barren as boulders women lie longing still
> To labour and love though they lay down long
>   ago.[39]

And there is a hint of that interest in and concern for
people as they are, in all their human individuality, which
appears again so strikingly in "The Hunchback in the
Park" and in *Under Milk Wood*. Another poem, apparently
written in 1938, in which Thomas had also gone back to
his childhood and in so doing had revealed a broader
feeling for humanity, is "After the Funeral" written in
memory of Ann Jones, "an ancient peasant aunt." In
1949 he was to say about this that it was the only poem he
had written "directly, about the life and death of one
particular human being I knew—and not about the very
many lives and deaths whether seen, as in my first poems,
in the tumultuous world of my own being or, as in the
later poems, in war, grief, and the great holes and corners
of universal love."[40] A poem of the same year which
belongs with "After the Funeral" is "The Tombstone
Told when she Died", which Thomas called "Hardy-
like". (Hardy was the poet of this century whom he most
admired.) Discussing with Vernon Watkins whether to
use the word "great" or the word "dear" in the last line
of the poem, Thomas said

> I wanted the girl's *terrible* reaction to orgastic [*sic*]
> death to be suddenly altered into a kind of despairing
> love. As I see it now, it strikes me as very moving. . . .[41]

and so it is:

> The tombstone told when she died.
> Her two surnames stopped me still. . . .

> I died before bedtime came
> But my womb was bellowing
> And I felt with my bare fall
> A blazing red harsh head tear up
> And the dear floods of his hair.[42]

Other poems collected in *The Map of Love* show Thomas moving towards both a more direct statement and a concern with life as it actually is rather than as conceived by a highly imaginative adolescent. There is the first of his birthday poems, "Twenty-four Years," with its sonorous and Whitmanesque concluding lines:

> In the final direction of the elementary town
> I advance for as long as forever is.[43]

There is a poem about what he was later to call his "craft or sullen art":

> On no work of words now for three lean months in
>   the bloody
> Belly of the rich year and the big purse of my body
> I bitterly take to task my poverty and craft;
> To take to give is all, return what is hungrily given
> Puffing the pounds of manna up through the dew to
>   heaven,
> The lovely gift of the gab bangs back on a blind
>   shaft.[44]

And there are five poems about his wife and their unborn child—"I Make this in a warring Absence," "Not from this Anger," "How shall my Animal," "A Saint about to Fall," and "If my Head hurt a hair's foot." "I Make this in a warring Absence," which was originally called "Poem for Caitlin," is, despite some incidental obscurities and something of the mechanically repetitive, metronomic rhythm of some of the earlier poems, as good a love-poem as all but the very best of our time—those of Yeats and Graves. The poem begins in "a warring absence" and ends in "a forgiving presence." That is to say, it is a poem, like the "Altarwise by Owl-Light" sonnet-sequence of *Twenty-five Poems*, in which there is a progression.

Thomas's liability to monotony of rhythm (which is less apparent in particular poems than it is in *18 Poems* and *Twenty-five Poems*) seems to be closely related to another defect of some of his early poems: their lack of any genuine progression. In lyrical poetry, progression, movement from a beginning to an ending, is not a virtue in itself, nor its absence a fault. Some of Thomas's early poems, however, seem to fail because in them the poet creates an illusion of a progression which is not actually there in the poems. "I Dreamed my Genesis,"[45] for example, appears to move from "I dreamed my genesis in sweat of sleep," through "I dreamed my genesis and died again," to "I dreamed my genesis in sweat of death." But the movement is apparent only. We deduce that there is intended to be a progression from "the sweat of sleep," i.e. conception and birth, through the "globe of heritage, journey | In bottom gear through night-geared man," *i.e.* the agonies of adolescence growing into manhood, and "the second death" of the sort of manhood men of Thomas's generation could expect, to "the sweat of death" itself. This is an intellectual paradigm of the poem. In the poem as we read it, the sweat all the way through (at least after the first stanza) is in fact the sweat of death—as can be seen in such phrases as "the measure of the worm," "Heir ... I | Rounded my globe of heritage," "and died again," "Sharp in my second death I marked the hills, harvest | Of hemlock and the blades." Once we are thus aware of the language and images employed in the poem, we are tempted to dismiss its ending as a mere nineteen-thirtyish gesture thrown in to finish the poem somehow because the poet has realised that he is in fact only saying the same thing over and over again:

> vision
> Of new man strength, I seek the sun.

In a similar way, the poem "Should Lanterns Shine,"[46] as it originally appeared in *New Verse*, had ended with the lines:

> Regard the moon, it hangs above the lawn;
> Regard the lawn, it lies beneath the moon.

Pointing out that the lines echo Eliot, and indirectly Laforgue, Vernon Watkins persuaded Thomas to delete them from the version in *Twenty-five Poems* and to end the poem with the two previous lines, which seem appropriately autobiographical:

> The ball I threw while playing in the park
> Has not yet reached the ground.

A sympathetic reading of the whole of Thomas's early poetry (by which I mean here *18 Poems* and *Twenty-five Poems*) shows that the comparative lack of rhythmical subtlety in some of the poems and the lack of any actual progression in those that pretend to it, are closely bound up with something else. Before we try to ascertain what that something else is, let us look at one other poem—one from the second volume. "A Grief ago" has been included in an influential modern anthology, *The Penguin Book of Contemporary Verse*; and its editor says of this poem that it is "full of towering phrases and with a real structure, but arbitrarily obscure for lack of a central theme or any clear impulse on the poet's part beyond that of wishing to produce a poem."[47] In other words (though the poem is perhaps more explicable than Allott suggests) this is a poem in which there is a great deal of linguistic and imagistic activity—but we are not sure what it is all about.

In some of the earlier poems, as in some of *The Map of Love* stories, we also get this impression of linguistic and imagistic activity, only to find that it all gets nowhere: the poem stops only because the poet is temporarily exhausted, though such in general is the verve of his rhythm and the exciting exactness of his language that it is only when we stop, because the poem has stopped, that we realise that we haven't got anywhere. An example of this is "The Seed-at-Zero"—in the last stanza we are just where we were in the first:

> The seed-at-zero shall not storm
> That town of ghosts, the trodden womb
> With her rampart to his tapping,
> No god-in-hero tumble down
> Dumbly and divinely stumbling
> Over the manwaging line. . . .
>
> Man-in-seed, in seed-at-zero,
> From the star-flanked fields of space,
> Thunders on the foreign town
> With a sand-bagged garrison,
> Nor the cannons of his kingdom
> Shall the hero-in-to-morrow
> Range from the grave-groping place.[48]

This tendency of the early poems to lack progression while pretending to it, a tendency which seems to be linked with the liability to rhythmical monotony, is, I have suggested, connected with something else. (The criticism, as has been shown, does not apply to poems like "If I were Tickled by the Rub of Love" and "Light Breaks where no Sun Shines"). What that something else is, is probably best put in Thomas's own words about all his early poems being perhaps part of one long poem: "I agree that each of my earlier poems might appear to constitute a section from one long poem."[49] We find striking corroboration of what at first might appear to be

a merely attitudinising statement on Thomas's part in
R. N. Maud's discovery that Thomas's first published
poem after leaving Swansea was an early version of
"And Death shall have no Dominion." The poem exists
in manuscript in the Dylan Thomas Collection of the
Lockwood Memorial Library of the University of Buffalo.
There it is poem "Twenty Three" in a notebook begun
on 1 Feb. 1933. As Maud says, the genesis of the poem
can be clearly seen in the crossed-out final lines of the
preceding poem in the notebook:

> Man's wants remain unsatisfied till death.
> Then, when his soul is naked, is he one
> With the man in the wind, and the west moon,
> With the harmonious thunder of the sun.[50]

What the one long poem might have been remains
hypothetical. It was so for Thomas himself, who made
the judgment looking back at his earlier work and trying
to assess its limitations. For us, his readers, now, Thomas's
statement has a double importance. Firstly, although the
observation seems originally to have been made by
Treece, Thomas with his usual gift for analysis of his own
poetry saw that it was a perceptive criticism. Secondly,
Thomas's admission that this was indeed so, is also an
admission that he had not yet at that time found himself
completely as a poet. G. S. Fraser makes some interesting
and pertinent remarks. "I hope I have conveyed my
impression—an impression which, when it first came
solidly home, very much surprised me—that in tone, in
style, in subject-matter Thomas is a much more various,
a much less narrowly consistent poet, and that in attitude
to life he is much more a developing poet, than people
make him out to be."[51] This is indeed true of Thomas's
work as a whole. With equal truth, Fraser says that "even
as late as 1939, Thomas's voice was still not always quite
his own. Or rather, he had his own voice, but he would
still from time to time try on other people's to see how

they fitted";[52] and he quotes two lines that, unless we know them, do not make us think of Dylan Thomas but rather of the general preoccupations of most of the poets of the nineteen-thirties:

> But wishes breed not, neither
> Can we fend off rock arrival. . . .[53]

Similarly, these lines might make us recall the war poets of 1914–18 before guessing that they were written by Dylan Thomas:

> shrapnel
> Rammed in the marching heart, hole
> In the stitched wound and clotted wind, muzzled
> Death on the mouth that ate the gas.[54]

It is one of Thomas's most extraordinary attributes that we do not notice these affinities and similarities until we look at the poems very closely. We should not be surprised that Thomas at times echoes other poets. Many young poets do so, and there is reason in Fraser's suggestion about Thomas's trying other people's voices. (Thomas was a skilled parodist, as is witnessed by various anecdotes, by his poem in homage to William Empson, and by the wickedly funny "How to be A Poet").

At the time he was writing these poems, Thomas was also writing prose, but a prose very different from his early efforts collected in *The Map of Love*. In March 1938, when he was still writing a story in the earlier manner (one that was to remain unfinished), "In the Direction of the Beginning," Thomas told Vernon Watkins that he had begun to work on a series of straightforward short stories about his native town, and in another letter later in the year he referred to these stories as "illuminated reporting."[55] These stories were published in 1940 as *Portrait of the Artist as a Young Dog*. Compared with the prose pieces of *The Map of Love*, the most obvious feature of these stories is that they are recognisably short stories.

D

Joyce was Thomas's most admired prose-writer, and although *Dubliners* made him depreciate his own stories, the idea of a volume of stories devoted to the town in which he had grown up obviously derives from Joyce's example. That Thomas himself was very well aware of this is shown not only by his ready acceptance of Richard Hughes's suggestion for the title, but also in the following postscript to a letter to Vernon Watkins:

> I'm so glad you liked the fresh, Dan story ["The Fight"]. I've finished the book now and have nothing to do but wait for Swansea, marble-town, city of laughter, little Dublin, home of at least 2 great men.[56]

Actually, Thomas's collection does not confine itself as rigorously to Swansea as Joyce's had confined itself to Dublin: the young dog is portrayed in the Carmarthenshire countryside as well as in his natal Swansea.

After the first two volumes of poetry and *The Map of Love*, the *Portrait* is, to begin with, something of a surprise. The three outstanding qualities of the stories in the *Portrait*, qualities which could hardly be guessed at from *18 Poems* and *Twenty-five Poems* and the prose and poems of *The Map of Love* are: a robust and all-embracing sense of humour, a remarkably accurate reporter's eye for the telling detail, and a wide compassion. It is less important that, as we know from the letters to Vernon Watkins and from the testimony of Daniel Jones, the stories of the *Portrait* are, as we might suspect merely from their collective title and from internal evidence, largely autobiographical.

"The Peaches" is an evocation of a childhood holiday —a holiday spent on a farm by a boy from a town, a "townee" in the country-boy's contemptuous idiom. In the story the farm is called Gorsehill—later, in a poem, Thomas was to call it Fern Hill—both names are evocative and apt. The aunt of the story was the Ann Jones whose "seventy years of stone" he had already celebrated in

a monstrous image blindly
Magnified out of praise.

In "The Peaches," she is "a little, brown-skinned, tooth-
less, hunchbacked woman with a cracked, sing-song
voice," and a drunken husband twice her size. The story
is localised, not merely in Wales, but in a particular part
of Wales, and the poignancy of the fiasco of the rich
friend's visit is all the more telling for that. The most
interesting thing in the story, however, is the character of
the narrator's cousin, Gwilym. Gwilym is a young man
who practises preaching:

> O God, Thou art everywhere all the time, in the dew
> of the morning, in the frost of the evening, in the field
> and the town, in the preacher and the sinner, in the
> sparrow and the big buzzard. Thou canst see every-
> thing, right down deep in our hearts; Thou canst see
> us when the sun is gone; Thou canst see us when there
> aren't any stars, in the gravy blackness, in the deep,
> deep, deep, deep pit; Thou canst see and spy and
> watch us all the time, in the little black corners, in the
> big cowboys' prairies, under the blankets when we're
> snoring fast, in the terrible shadows, pitch black, pitch
> black; Thou canst see everything we do, in the night
> and the day, in the day and the night, everything,
> everything; Thou canst see all the time. O God, mun,
> you're like a bloody cat.[57]

Such a passage shows conclusively that, however much
Thomas may have admired Joyce, the prose-writer he
was most indebted to was another Welshman, Caradoc
Evans. This extraordinary and too-little-known writer
has been justly called by Professor Gwyn Jones "the
daddy of the Anglo-Welsh," and more politely by
Aneirin Talfan Davies "the father of modern Anglo-
Welsh literature." Caradoc Evans, a monoglot Welshman
until he crossed the border, was almost completely a

product of the Welsh Sunday-school, brought up on the Welsh Bible and the poetry and rhetoric of the Welsh pulpit. He reacted violently against what he regarded as the Pharisaism and hypocrisy of Welsh chapel-goers, but when he came to express this revolt in words he could only do so in an extraordinary prose based on the rhythms and idioms of Welsh nonconformity; a virile, exuberant, non-conforming prose that has influenced almost every subsequent Anglo-Welsh writer, and not least Dylan Thomas.

Cousin Gwilym in "The Peaches" sermonises just in the vein of the D.D. from Aberbedw in Caradoc's story "Pews for Saints and Fire for Sinners, but no Rest for the Soulless":

People, where are you off to? Hell sinners, ha-ho? Heaven godlers, ha-ho? Sinners will slip like sweating badgers through the belly of the earth to Hell. What then? Some will be thrown under the fire, some into it, some on top. They will burn wherever they are. The fire will burst their toes and hands and eyes. These things will grow again and the fire will burst them again, and so on till the last spark in fire Hell is the first of the new fire. This is the everlasting fire Matthew Apostol speaks of.[58]

"The Peaches," with Uncle Jim, who sells his live-stock to go on the drink, and Cousin Gwilym, who has sex and religion, actresses and sermons, inextricably mixed up in his mind, is a very funny story. It is also, in its understated realisation of the havoc that financial and social differences can make to childish friendships, a sad and touching story, comparable in this respect to such poems as "Paper and Sticks" and "The Hunchback in the Park" and to the presentation of Lily Smalls and Bessy Bighead in *Under Milk Wood*. "A Visit to Grandpa's" is, at first sight, uproariously funny, and funny only— the old man who drives horses in his bed at night, but is cunning enough to say to his grandson next day, "If you heard those old birds in the night, you'd wake me up and say there were horses in the trees," who drives his "short, weak pony" to Llanstephan as if it were a bison, and who doesn't want to be buried in Llanstephan but in Llangadock where "The ground is comfy . . . you can twitch your legs without putting them in the sea." Funny as the story is, the more one reads it the more one becomes aware that it is informed by the same understanding compassion for the aged as the poem in memory of Ann Jones and the two poems for the poet's father. There is a sad dignity about the old man at the end of the story:

> But Grandpa stood firmly on the bridge, and clutched his bag to his side, and stared at the flowing river and the sky, like a prophet who has no doubt.[59]

Three other stories, "Patricia, Edith, and Arnold," "Extraordinary Little Cough," and "Who do you Wish was with us," reveal Thomas's remarkable ability to enter with sympathy, but without either condescension or mawkishness, into the lives of other people—servant-girls discovering they both have the same undeserving suitor, the boy who runs five miles on the beach at night because of the unmeant challenge of two bullies, the young man whose life has been spent in nursing his sick parents and brother.

The remainder of the stories in the *Portrait* are more directly autobiographical. "The Fight," records Thomas's first meeting with his friend, Daniel Jones. "Where Tawe Flows," "Old Garbo," and "One Warm Saturday," and, less explicitly, "Just like Little Dogs," are the real "young dog" stories—stories of the young, naïve, expectant provincial reporter who is one day going to go to London and become a famous writer.

"I'll put them all in a story by and by," says the young reporter to Mr Farr at the end of "Old Garbo"; and this, of course, is just what Dylan Thomas did. And when he did, his brief training as a reporter stood him in good stead: he presents us equally well with the small, significant details:

> She was a thin woman with bitter lines, tired hands, the ruins of fine brown eyes, and a superior nose[60]

and with the large, general picture:

> I made my way through the crowds: the Valley men, up for the football; the country shoppers; the window gazers; the silent, shabby men at the corners of the packed streets, standing in isolation in the rain; the press of mothers and prams; old women in black, brooched dresses carrying frails; smart girls with shining mackintoshes and splashed stockings; little, dandy lascars, bewildered by the weather; business men with wet spats; through a mushroom forest of umbrellas; and all the time I thought of the paragraphs I would never write. I'll put you all in a story by and by.[61]

Two stories written many years later belong so obviously to the *genre* of the *Portrait* that they must be mentioned along with it. These are "The Followers," first published in 1952, and "A Story," which Thomas read on television in 1953. (Both stories are now printed in *A Prospect of the Sea*). "The Followers" is very similar in theme and tone to "Just like Little Dogs," a wry recollection of urban adolescence. "A Story" is Thomas's most exuberant and uninhibited piece of sheer fun, with none of the overtones of irony or sadness that qualify the humour of the *Portrait* stories. Here again we meet the poet's enormous and drunken uncle "too big for everything except the great black boats of his boots," and his aunt (Ann Jones) who was "so small she could hit him only if she stood on a chair, and every Saturday night at half past ten he would lift her up, under his arm, on to a chair in the kitchen so that she could hit him on the head with whatever was handy, which was always a china dog"; and the whole glorious crowd, Will Sentry, old O. Jones, and the rest, who embark on the charabanc outing to Porthcawl which they never reach:

> And dusk came down warm and gentle on thirty wild, wet, pickled, splashing men without a care in the world at the end of the world in the west of Wales. And, "Who goes there?" called Will Sentry to a wild duck flying.[62]

Though the *Portrait* was published in 1940 and *The Map of Love* in 1939, there was a certain amount of overlapping in the writing of them. 1939 was a crucial year for Thomas in more ways than one: the war which he dreaded and hated began; he became the father of a son, Llewelyn; and his writing, both in poetry and prose, was beginning to develop in new directions. Marriage, fatherhood, war: the young poet was beginning to find that life was both more complex and more terrifying than he had envisaged it could be for him. The new realisations and responsibilities left their mark on his writing. One of the important poems in *The Map of Love* is "A Saint about to Fall," which was originally entitled at Vernon Watkins's suggestion "Poem in the Ninth Month." The Watkins title makes quite clear what is deducible, though perhaps not immediately obvious, from the poem itself—that it is written in anticipation of the birth of his first child. The complex of feelings of a humane, sensitive, and loving man whose child is about to be born in the year when the inevitable war "that would never happen again" broke out, is powerfully and agonisedly expressed:

> Lapped among herods wail
> As their blade marches in
> That the eyes are already murdered,
> The stocked heart is forced, and agony has another
>   mouth to feed.[63]

Thomas had, in fact, provisionally called this poem "In September" and "that at all only because it was a terrible war month"—it was, he said, "a poem written to a child about to be born . . . and telling it what a world it will see, what horrors and hells."[64] Because of its very concentration on the subjective situation of a man, a particular man, about to become a father at that moment in history, the poem today reads as a more eloquent example of civilised man's instinctive protest against war than many more overtly propagandist poems of the time. But this is not the most important aspect of the poem. What that is, was explicitly stated by Thomas in his letter to Vernon Watkins:

> It's an optimistic, taking-everything, poem. The two most important words are "Cry Joy".[65]

The words begin the last four lines of the poem:

> Cry joy that this witchlike midwife second
> Bullies into rough seas you so gentle
> And makes with a flick of the thumb and sun
> A thundering bullring of your silent and girl-circled
>   island.[66]

The importance of the words "Cry joy" draws our attention to a singular feature of Thomas's poetry: it is optimistic, or at least celebratory. Most of the poetry of this century that is worth re-reading is understandably and expectedly pessimistic or tragic. Thomas himself, as his letters and poems show, was well aware of the "horrors & hells" of the world in which he lived. (According to Brinnin, he once claimed to have seen the gates of hell,[67] and as far as I know there is no valid reason for disbelieving Thomas.) We can scarcely call his early poems cheerful, but on the other hand neither are they professionally grim in the standard manner of the nineteen-thirties. And more and more as he matured do the notes of exultation and celebration, first heard clearly in the poem in memory of Ann Jones, become dominant in his poetry.

He has been, especially by American critics, compared to Whitman. There is some validity in the comparison, as he himself was comically aware. In 1940 he sent Vernon Watkins a 100-line satirical poem, "The Countryman's Return," which he described as a "half comic attack on myself . . . this middle-class, beardless Walt who props humanity, in his dirty, weeping, expansive moments, against corners and counters and tries to slip, in grand delusions of all embracing humanitarianism, everyone into himself."[68] But Louis MacNeice was nearer the mark when he said that no poet of our time was a better example than Dylan Thomas of Yeats's description of the poet as one who knows that "Hamlet and Lear are gay."[69] Thomas's unique ability to find proper reason for celebration and exultation in the contemporary world of "horrors & hells" is most succinctly expressed in Polly Garter's famous remark, "Oh, isn't life a terrible thing, thank God?"—a remark that looks merely silly quoted on its own and out of context like that, but which in its context is both moving and meaningful.

"Cry joy," Thomas said, were the most important words in the most personally urgent poem he had written to date and one written in a desperate time. And at the untimely time of his death, he was working on what was to be his loudest cry of joy, the ambitiously-conceived long poem, "In Country Heaven."

REFERENCES

1. H. G. Porteous, "Map of Llareggub," in Tedlock, p. 94.
2. Richard Hughes, in a letter to the author.
3. *Letters*, p. 20.
4. *Prospect*, p. 75.
5. *Loc. cit.*, pp. 93–4.
6. A. Talfan Davies, "A Question of Language," in *Yr*

Einion, v (1953), p. 23. "The Tree" in *Prospect,* p. 47.

7. "A Prospect of the Sea," in *Prospect,* p. 8.

8. "The Burning Baby" in *Contemporary Poetry and Prose,* 1 (1936), pp. 10–14. "The School for Witches," *ibid.,* 4/5 (1936), pp. 95–100.

9. *Portrait,* pp. 40–51.

10. *Prospect,* pp. 3–12.

11. *Loc. cit.,* pp. 20–4.

12. *Loc. cit.,* pp. 25–34.

13. *Loc. cit.,* pp. 51–7.

14. *Loc. cit.,* pp. 35–41.

15. *Loc. cit.,* pp. 78–81.

16. "The Orchards," in *Prospect,* p. 85.

17. In *Prospect,* p. 79.

18. *Q.E.O.M.,* p. 130.

19. R. N. Maud, "Dylan Thomas's Poetry," in *Essays in Criticism,* IV (1954), 413.

20. *C.P.,* p. 9.

21. *C.P.,* p. 7.

22. *Swansea Grammar School Magazine,* Apr. 1931, p. 141.

23. John Arlott, "Dylan Thomas and Broadcasting," in *The Adelphi,* XXX (1954), 121.

24. "Now," in *C.P.,* p. 51.

25. "Ears in the Turrets Hear," in *C.P.,* p. 58.

26. "The Hand that Signed the Paper," in *C.P.,* p. 62.

27. "I have Longed to Move away," in *C.P.,* p. 64.

28. Francis Scarfe, "Dylan Thomas: A Pioneer," in Tedlock, p. 102.

29. Olson, *The Poetry of Dylan Thomas,* p. 64.

30. J. A. Rolph, *Dylan Thomas: A Bibliography,* London 1956, p. 11.

31. *C.P.,* p. 71.

32. *C.P.,* p. 76.

33. Augustus John, *The Monogamous Bohemian,* in *Adam International Review,* 238 (1953), p. 9.

34. Richard Hughes, in a letter to the author.

35. *Letters,* p. 27.

36. Brinnin, *Dylan Thomas in America,* p. 62.

37. *Letters,* p. 21.

38. *C.P.,* p. 89.

39. *C.P.,* p. 176.

40. "On Reading one's own Poems," in *Q.E.O.M.,* p. 137.

41. *Letters,* p. 44.

42. "The Tombstone Told," in *C.P.,* p. 93.

43. "Twenty-four Years," in *C.P.,* p. 99.

44. "On no work of words," in *C.P.,* p. 94.

45. *C.P.,* p. 28.

46. *C.P.,* p. 63.

47. Kenneth Allott, in *The Penguin Book of Contemporary Verse,* p. 225.

48. "The Seed-at-Zero," in *C.P.,* pp. 42–3.

49. Henry Treece, *Dylan Thomas,* London 1949, p. 48.

50. R. N. Maud, "Dylan Thomas's first published Poem," in *M.L.N.,* LXXIV (1959), 117.

51. G. S. Fraser, *Dylan Thomas,* in "Writers and their Work," London 1957, p. 21.

52. Fraser, *op. cit.,* p. 20.

53. "We lying by seasand," in *C.P.*, p. 82.

54. "I dreamed my genesis," in *C.P.*, p. 28.

55. *Letters*, pp. 39, 47.

56. *Letters*, p. 77.

57. "The Peaches," in *Portrait*, pp. 21–2.

58. Caradoc Evans, *Pilgrims in a Foreign Land*, London 1942, p. 128.

59. *Portrait*, p. 51.

60. "Where Tawe Flows," in *Portrait*, pp. 137–8.

61. "Old Garbo," in *Portrait*, pp. 186–7.

62. "A Story," in *Prospect*, pp. 127–36.

63. *C.P.*, pp. 95–6.

64. *Letters*, p. 45.

65. *Loc. cit.*, p. 45.

66. *C.P.*, p. 96.

67. Brinnin, *Dylan Thomas in America*, p. 211.

68. *Letters*, p. 85.

69. Louis MacNeice, in Tedlock, p. 85.

CHAPTER III

LONDON AND WAR

The outbreak of war shocked and sickened, and to a certain extent silenced, Dylan Thomas. It was not that he was more sensitive than other young poets who were not shocked and sickened in the same way. Auden and others had been warning their generation of the imminence and horror of war for a decade; and if it is not true that Yeats's "The Second Coming"[1] was the favourite poem of this generation (there was, after all, *The Waste Land* as well), it is certainly true that Yeats's poem expressed their typical feeling about the all too probable future. On the other hand, to the younger generation of poets growing up in the nineteen-thirties—some of the best of whom, such as Keith Douglas, Sidney Keyes, and Alun Lewis, were to be killed in action like their predecessors, Wilfred Owen and Edward Thomas—the War was something expected and inevitable.

Dylan Thomas's attitude was more complex than it at first appears to be. It was the inevitable outcome of the inherent attitude to life that Thomas had been assiduously cultivating since his schooldays. Though full of human sympathy and very much aware of the social realities of contemporary Britain, Thomas was the least politically-minded of poets. Augustus John records that Thomas once told him that he had joined the Communist Party, but left it when he discovered that he was expected to turn his poetic gifts to propagandist purposes. Whether he actually joined the Party for a short time or was merely pulling his venerable compatriot's leg (which he was very capable of doing) is immaterial. The War was for Thomas the ultimate representation of those aspects of life which he had to reject because he could not cope with them. But whereas against the stupidities of society he could erect barriers of buffoonery, drink, and ostentatiously anti-social behaviour, such defences were of no use against the brute fact of war. As a result, his behaviour was very confused.

In August 1939 the prospect of war was filling him with "horror & terror & lassitude."[2] As for the War itself, and its effects on him, the story is best told in the words of his closest friend, Vernon Watkins:

> The advent of war filled Dylan with horror, and the war itself was a nightmare from which he never completely recovered. But for a tribunal at which he had to be a witness he would certainly have asked to be registered as a conscientious objector; but the attitude of the conscientious objectors themselves had also impressed him: he would never, he said, object on religious grounds. So he registered for the Army, 'as a never-fighter', as he put it in one of the letters which is not here.[3]

As it happened, he was medically unfit.

According to Rayner Heppenstall, shortly after the outbreak of war, Thomas attempted to organise a writers' manifesto against war, to be printed in some "widely circulated popular literary magazine. . . ." Heppenstall protested that perhaps it was "the writer's duty to undergo contemporary reality at its most extreme," to which Thomas replied in a letter dated 2 Nov. 1939:

> When you come to talk about one's duty as a writer, then *one* can only say that his duty is to write. If to undergo contemporary reality to its most extreme is to join in a war . . . against people you do not know, and probably to be killed or maimed, then one can only say

flippantly that the best poems about death were always written when the poets were alive, that Lorca didn't have to be gored before writing a bullsong, that for a writer to undergo the utmost reality of poverty is for him to starve to death, and therefore to be, as a writer, useless. . . . The matey folk-warmth of the trenches can only make for hysterical friendships, do or die companionships, the joking desperate homosexual propinquity of those about to die: the joy of living and dying with a Saturday football crowd on an exploding ground.[4]

There are two other explicit statements of Thomas's attitude to war. The first of these is in a letter written in 1945 to Oscar Williams, who had sent Thomas a copy of his anthology of war poetry:

War can't produce poetry, only poets can, and war can't produce poets either because they bring themselves up in such a war that this outward bang bang of men against men is something they have passed a long time ago on their poems' way towards peace. A poet writing a poem is at peace with everything except words, which are eternal actions; only in the lulls between the warring work on words can he be at war with man. Poets can stop bullets, but bullets can't stop poets. What is a poet anyway? He is a man who has written or is writing what he, in his utmost human fallible integrity, necessarily communal, believes to be good poetry. As he writes good poetry very rarely, he is most often at peace with the eternal actions of words and is therefore very likely to be caught up in any bang bang that is going. When he is fighting he is not a poet. Nor is a craftsman a craftsman. I think capital-lettered War can only in subject matter affect poetry. Violence and suffering are all the time, and it does not matter how you are brought up against them.[5]

In the following year, Thomas was saying the same sort of thing more publicly in a broadcast on Wilfred Owen:

And this time, when, in the words of an American critic, the audiences of the earth, witnessing what well may be the last act of their own tragedy, insist upon chief actors who are senseless enough to perform a cataclysm, the voice of the poetry of Wilfred Owen speaks to us, down the revolving stages of thirty years, with terrible new significance and strength. We had not forgotten his poetry, but perhaps we had allowed ourselves to think of it as the voice of one particular time, one place, one war. Now, at the beginning of what, in the future, may never be known to historians as the 'atomic age'—for obvious reasons: there may be no historians—we can see, re-reading Owen, that he is a poet of all times, all places, and all wars. There is only one war: that of men against men.[6]

In 1940 the Thomases left Laugharne. They lived for a while in Oxfordshire and in Wiltshire, and then in London, where they remained, except for brief spells back in Laugharne and in New Quay, for the duration of the War. After his early enchanted spell there, Thomas both hated London and was fascinated by it: hated it because he could not find there the necessary peace in which he could write his poems; was fascinated by it because of the pubs and clubs and friends and acquaintances he could find there. He once called it "the Capital punishment."[7] In 1941 we find him, penniless and without a job, describing London to Vernon Watkins as "stinking, friendless," a place where he and Caitlin "sit in our bedroom and think with hate of the people who can go to restaurants."[8] That this was not merely a passing fit of irritation induced by circumstances is indicated by a letter he wrote to Oscar Williams in 1953 describing his arrival back in London after an American tour:

... I weak-wormed through festoons, bunting, flags, great roses, sad spangles, paste and tinsel, the million cardboard simpers and ogrish plaster statuettes of the queen, I crawled as early as sin in the chilly weeping morning through the city's hushed hangover and all those miles of orange-peel, nibbled sandwiches, broken bottles, discarded vests, vomit and condoms, lollipops, senile fish, blood, lips, old towels, teeth, turds, soiled blowing newspapers by the unread mountains, all the spatter and bloody gravy and giant mousiness that go to show how a loyal and phlegmatic people—'London can break it!'—enjoyed themselves like hell the day before.[9]

Since he was Dylan Thomas, the next sentence in the letter is "And, my God, wouldn't I have enjoyed it too." But the tone of the letter amply demonstrates the truth of Vernon Watkins's statement:

The calmest and happiest days of his life were probably those he spent in Wales. The chief part of his creative writing was done in the landscape and among the people to whom he was most deeply attached.[10]

In London, as in America later, there were too many distractions and temptations of a kind to which he too easily succumbed.

It was during those confused, unhappy years in wartime London, while he was working in films and radio, that the "Dylan Legend," later to be amplified, exaggerated, and distorted in America, really began to grow. Naturally enough, Thomas in London had many friends and more acquaintances. Furthermore, his own temperament and the nature of the work he was doing reacted on each other. Thomas was never, as some people thought, a *naïf* as far as poetry was concerned; but in many respects, as far as society, especially metropolitan society, was concerned, he remained a *naïf* all his life—not too unlike his own Samuel Bennet. Both his wartime life in London and his later experiences in America bear regrettable witness to this.

In his foreword to Thomas's unfinished picaresque novel, *Adventures in the Skin Trade*, Vernon Watkins wonders why Thomas abandoned the book after writing only four chapters, especially since Thomas wrote easily and rapidly in this comic vein and "it exercised his gift for entertaining others and interesting himself at the same time." Watkins suggests that a possible reason was the poet's distrust of his own facility; but "A more likely reason is, I think, the impact of war, and particularly of the London air raids, on his appalled and essentially tragic vision."

To talk of Thomas's essentially tragic vision would seem to be contradictory of what I have said earlier about the sense of joy and exultation that informs his poetry, its essentially celebratory nature. The contradiction is rather a paradox, the paradox of Yeats's "Hamlet and Lear are gay." In one of the few intelligent discussions of Thomas's prose, D. C. Muecke finds that, although there is a fundamentally tragic theme, "the pity and terror of irreversible time, ineluctable death," in all Thomas's prose, this theme is not all-important:

> at least equally important and much more obvious, [is] his passionate and total apprehension of the world about him. Again, like Shakespeare, his feeling for what was tragic in this world was strong in proportion to what was perhaps largely its cause, his love of the multitudinary world.[11]

Thomas himself expressed this directly in "Poem on his Birthday":

> And this last blessing most
>
> That the closer I move
> To death, one man through his sundered hulks,

E

The louder the sun blooms
And the tusked, ramshackling sea exults. . . .[12]

Whatever terms we may use by way of explanation, the fact is that Thomas wrote very little poetry between 1941 and 1945. In effect, he wrote only one important poem ("Ceremony after a Fire Raid") in four years. Despite this, with the publication of *Deaths and Entrances* in 1946, it became apparent, except to austerity-conditioned scrutineers and determined lookers-at-objects, that the precocious, wilful, obscure boy genius of *18 Poems* and *Twenty-five Poems*, "the Rimbaud of Cwmdonkin Drive," as he took malicious delight in describing himself, had developed into a serious and mature artist in beautiful control (most of the time) of his rhythms, his images, and his words. A critical discussion of Thomas's poetry must centre on *Deaths and Entrances*. There had been good poems in the three previous volumes, and some of the best were still to come, but *Deaths and Entrances* is the core of Thomas's poetic achievement.

At the end of his foreword to *Adventures in the Skin Trade*, Vernon Watkins, referring to the fact that as late as June 1953 Thomas was writing to Oscar Williams about going on with the projected novel, says:

As it was, at the time when he stopped writing these pages, the pressure of the anarchy of war itself and the vision of distorted London took the place of his half-fictional vision and compelled his imagination forward to the 'Ceremony After a Fire Raid', and to the beautiful poems evoking childhood, 'It was My Thirtieth Year to Heaven' and 'Fern Hill'. He could still go back to peace, but from there he could no longer go forward.[13]

Taking a clue from this statement by his fellow-poet and closest friend we may separate the poems in the volume into three not altogether arbitrary categories: there are the "human interest" poems like "Paper and Sticks" and "The Hunchback in the Park"; there are the poems dealing directly with the experience of war; and there are the new poems on a big scale, "Vision and Prayer," "Ballad of the Long-legged Bait," and "A Winter's Tale." This classification is, admittedly, rough and ready, and not all the poems in the volume fit into it.

Thomas wrote only four poems about the War: "A Refusal to Mourn the Death, by Fire, of a Child in London," "Deaths and Entrances," "Ceremony after a Fire Raid," and "Dawn Raid." It is noticeable that all four deal with the one aspect of the War of which Thomas had direct, personal experience, the air-raids on London; and that they all deal with this aspect from the one point of view with which Thomas was familiar—that of the more or less helpless civilian having willy-nilly to undergo the agonies and terrors of such an experience. Not the least of Thomas's virtues as a poet was that he knew his limitations. It would be impertinent to point out that, apart from some film work, he made no attempt at writing propaganda, either patriotic or anti-war, had he not deliberately drawn attention to the fact himself in the title of the finest of his shorter poems, "A Refusal to Mourn the Death, by Fire, of a Child in London." Nor did Thomas make any attempt to write about other conditions of war of which he could in the nature of things know nothing or only by hearsay and at second-hand. His few war poems were obstinately and magnificently civilian.

The least successful of the war poems is "Dawn Raid." If it is more than "a string of fantastic conceits,"[14] it is not much more. We have a newspaper headline title which the poem hardly develops or enlarges on at all. Certainly, the rest of the poem does not live up to the promise of the simple and moving opening lines:

When the morning was waking over the war
He put on his clothes and stepped out and he died.[15]

Olson very pertinently compares Thomas the poet with Thomas the prose-writer, and says that the former has genius, the latter merely a high degree of competence. Olson may be less than just to Thomas the prose-writer in saying this; but he goes on to make some very perceptive remarks about Thomas as a writer of both prose and poetry. Pointing out that Thomas the prose-writer is much more versatile than Thomas the poet, Olson says:

The prose-writer assumes many characters, devises many situations, plays upon emotions which range from the serious to the comic. The poet assumes a single character; and, strictly speaking, he is a poet only of the most exalted emotions, the most exalted grief or joy.[16]

Olson's further statement about Thomas the poet has equally obvious truth:

Thomas' imagination could transport him anywhere, through all space and all time: but it is also true that, wherever it takes him, he sees nothing but himself. He can enter into worm and animal, but he will look out through his own eyes. He can create worlds; but he creates worlds in his own image, and remains the centre of his own thought and feeling.[17]

Two of Thomas's war poems deal with the death of individuals—one, that of a child, the other, that of a very old man. "Dawn Raid" is a failure; "A Refusal to Mourn" comes off magnificently. In both poems we have what Olson calls a "curiously external view of death": there is no attempt by the poet to enter into the feelings of the child or the old man. What then, is the difference between the two poems? Why is one a failure and one a plangent success? In "Dawn Raid" Thomas is merely telling us, with all the flamboyant and rhythmical rhetoric of which he is capable, what he has already told us in the adequately simple words of the title. It is merely the bizarre nature of the incident itself that the poet appears to be interested in and is drawing our attention to. Reading the poem, one is compelled to imagine the commonsense, cynical, or even callous comments of the surviving inhabitants of the street in which the centenarian died. But in "A Refusal to Mourn" the poet himself is deeply involved, and so therefore are his readers. Olson points out, quite rightly, that the poem is about Thomas, not about the dead child. (The same point is implicit in Empson's comment.) But this is not a fault—it merely means that the poem is of the same kind as *Lycidas*, which is really about the young John Milton, not its ostensible subject, the drowned Edward King. "A Refusal to Mourn" (which has been sympathetically examined by a number of critics, including David Daiches and William Empson) is a statement of the poet's refusal to make propaganda out of the child's death, deeply moving though that death is. Its paraphrasable meaning reads something like this: "I shall never, until the end of the world and the return of all things to their primal elements, distort the meaning of this child's death by mourning for her. One dies but once, and through that death becomes reunited with the timeless unity of all things." This meaning is reinforced and expanded and enriched by the rhythm and imagery of the poem. Thomas employs a basically iambic line, varied by inversions and extra syllables; the movement, despite the scarcity of punctuation, is fittingly slow and solemn; and the metrical variations are semantically justified, as in the lines

Tells with silence the last light breaking. . . .

Deep with the first dead lies London's daughter. . . .

The grains beyond age, the dark veins of her
    mother. . . .[18]

The language and imagery of the poem are sacramental and Biblical: "Zion of the water bead | And the synagogue of the ear of corn," "valley of sackcloth," "blaspheme down the stations of the breath." Thomas is making a profoundly serious statement about a very moving subject (the death of the child) which is part of a larger theme (death in general). He shows his own seriousness about the subject, and enables us to share that seriousness, by his choice of words and images and his control of rhyme and rhythm—avoiding the conventional, yet fixing our attention by definite pattern; shocking us into awareness of his meaning ("A Refusal to Mourn" and "a grave truth") without distracting us by technical or linguistic virtuosity.

In the earlier poems Thomas had displayed an astonishing imaginative ability to project himself into the world of the embryo and the womb. Now, in "Paper and Sticks" and "The Hunchback in the Park," he shows himself capable of the dramatic realisation of other people (there had already been something of this in "After the Funeral," but Ann Jones, whose "scrubbed and sour humble hands | Lie with religion in their cramp," shares the poem with the mourner, the "desolate boy who slits his throat | In the dark of the coffin and sheds dry leaves"). "The Hunchback in the Park" is Thomas's most successful non-subjective poem. We are presented here with a character, a person in a scene, a setting. (We learn from "Reminiscences of Childhood" that there really was a hunchback in Cwmdonkin Park when Thomas was a boy.)[19] The poem, which at first sight is one of the most obviously straightforward that Thomas ever wrote, is very subtly constructed. The few details that we are given about the hunchback—that he is solitary, that he eats bread from a newspaper, that he drinks water from the chained cup of the fountain, that he sleeps at night in a dogkennel—these details add up to the information that he is a tramp, a vagrant, a homeless outcast, not a normal member of society. He is in fact doubly an outcast, because of his deformity as well as of his vagrancy, and therefore an object of mockery to the truant boys playing in the park. This pathetic figure whose anonymity, solitariness, and outcast nature are emphasised by the term "a . . . mister," "Made all day until bell time | A woman figure without fault | . . . That she might stand in the night | . . . All night in the unmade park." There are two small puzzles in the poem. The hunchback is "propped between trees and water," that is, he is in the park

> From the opening of the garden lock
> That lets the trees and water enter
> Until the Sunday sombre bell at dark. . . .[20]

(Thomas uses a similar conceit in "Fern Hill").

This is a clue to what is happening in the poem: everything is seen through a child's eye. In effect, the unwritten stage-direction to the poem says, "This is the way it was, or this is the way things seemed, when I was a child." The other small puzzle, which also turns out to be a clue to the poem's interpretation, occurs in the description of the park as "unmade." "Unmade" is the opposite of "made," and what is made in the poem is the figure of the woman in the hunchback's mind. The park, then, is "unmade" in the sense that it is not the product of the hunchback's mind, but something external, actually there. Why does the hunchback have the woman figure standing in the park all night, instead of taking her to his dogkennel bed? Because the park is preferable to his dogkennel, the park is his habitat; locking it up at night, which means locking him out of it, is a deprivation—he, as it were, retains it in some way by sending or placing his imaginary figure there when he cannot be there himself. This does not contradict the conceit of the locked park going away at night—the park goes away for the child, through whose eyes we see all this; it does not go away for the hunchback. The structure of the poem may be represented by three concentric circles: the outermost, enclosing one, is the poet's present vision of the child he used to be; the intermediate one is that child's vision of the park and the hunchback; the central one is the dream of the hunchback.

In a poem like this, with its careful use of structure and its beautifully economic precision of phrase and image, we can see that the statement Thomas made in a long and often-quoted letter to Henry Treece about his method of composition is in certain respects misleading, particularly in regard to his later poetry. Replying to Treece's criticism of the diffuseness of his early poems, Thomas wrote:

> A poem by myself *needs* a host of images, because its centre is a host of images. I make one image—though 'make' is not the word; I let, perhaps, an image be 'made' emotionally in me and then apply to it what intellectual and critical forces I possess—let it breed another, let that image contradict the first, make, of the third image bred out of the other two together, a fourth contradictory image, and let them all, within my imposed formal limits, conflict. . . .[21]

The length and earnestness and confused imagery of the whole explanation are evidence enough that Thomas was here trying seriously to explain, to himself even more than to others, how he wrote his poems. (Treece does not give a date for the letter, but the book was published in 1949.) Glimpses of the poet actually at work are provided by Brinnin and Watkins and by the worksheets of "Poem on his Birthday" reproduced in *Poetry* (Chicago) in November 1955. When Brinnin was staying with Thomas in Laugharne in 1951, he noticed that whenever Thomas made a manuscript revision, however minor, to a poem, he would then copy out the whole poem in longhand. He showed Brinnin more than two hundred "separate and distinct" versions of "Fern Hill." The poet's verbal explanation of this laborious method is perhaps a clearer statement of how his poems were written than the long, confused letter to Treece. Almost all his poems originated in a "given" phrase; if the phrase was right, it suggested another, and in this way the poem would "accumulate" within the pattern of his "imposed formal limits." The constant recopying that accompanied his revisions was, he explained, his way of "keeping the poem together"— he saw the process of a poem's growth as organic.[22] Watkins gives a similar account to Brinnin's of how Thomas built up a poem phrase by phrase.[23]

This explanation of his working methods does, however, underplay the application to the "given," the originating word or phrase or image, of "what intellectual and critical forces I possess." Although, as Watkins finely says, "he recognised at all times that it was for the sake of divine accidents that a poem existed at all," he devoted a great deal of care to the actual construction of a poem. Particularly, he was devoted to, one might almost say obsessed by, the idea of symmetry in the parts of a poem. The outstanding examples of this are "Vision and Prayer" with its lozenge- and hourglass-shaped verses in the first and second parts respectively, and the "Author's Prologue," in which the second fifty-two lines rhyme in reverse order with the first fifty-two. The craftsman's motive that drove him to such an extreme was also responsible for his fondness for such difficult traditional verse-forms as the sonnet and the villanelle, and for his constant, laborious search for the right word, the exact image. In the first (and on the whole, regrettable) book written on Dylan Thomas, Henry Treece said that "Thomas's poems seem to proceed by a simple associative mechanism, controlled by his rhythmic scheme and fed by his cultural and verbal habits."[24] The suggestion has been repeated by other critics, especially hostile ones. The *Letters to Vernon Watkins*, with their revelation of

Thomas's critical perception and his readiness to accept suggested amendments to his own poems unless they conflicted with his conception of the poem, are in themselves sufficient refutation of this criticism which would make Thomas out to be a sort of surrealist, a hit-or-miss automatic writer. To the evidence of the *Letters* we can add that of his manuscripts. In November 1955, *Poetry* (Chicago) reproduced eight holograph pages of "Poem on his Birthday." Here we see "the rhymer in the long tongued room" working towards the lines that finally became

> small fishes glide
> Through wynds and shells of drowned
> Ship towns to pastures of otters.[25]

Unsatisfied with his first versions of these lines, Thomas listed the following alternatives before deciding on their final wording: "Acres, Boroughs, Harbours, Dwellings, Quarters, Arbours, Lair, Buildings, Tenements, Alleys, Galleries, Cellars, Bowers, Seals, Lap; Arks, Dens, Cells, Courts, Wynds, Lanes, Wharves, Quays, Docks, Roads, Halls, vaults, farms." This exhaustive testing of possible alternatives is scarcely evidence of a compulsory associative verbal mechanism. As the American critic, Cid Corman, said after studying the drafts of a poem by Thomas: "I know that his seeming spontaneity is a studied grace. Rhetoric is his controlling artifice. . . . His drafts are many and also the metamorphoses. They testify to a keen critical self-scrutiny and an ear that will not work without the mind."[26]

What *Deaths and Entrances* also made clear was that Thomas was essentially a religious poet. Perhaps the first person to observe this had been, naturally enough, Vernon Watkins, himself, as he notes, a religious poet and like Thomas without "aptitude for political reform." Thomas's early poetry had been full of words, names, puns, and images from the Bible and Welsh nonconformity—Jordan, cross, Christ, thorny, sunday faced, bred of Adam, hallowed, manna, in the beginning, angelic, genesis, the worm, "second | Rise of the skeleton and | Rerobing of the naked ghost," Eloi, devil, sin, Lazarus, Jacob, "a talking snake," Eden, Jericho, Job, "the grave sin-eater," "like exodus a chapter from the garden." The reader of the early poems could be forgiven for assuming that Thomas used such language and imagery because they were available to him rather than for any specifically religious purposes. Even among the early poems, however, there are a few which are specifically and overtly religious—Christian, though not sectarian. Particularly, there are "This Bread I Break," "And Death shall have no Dominion," and the "Altarwise by Owl-Light" sonnet-sequence.

In *Deaths and Entrances* the central religious concern, which had been in the main latent or obscured, becomes quite overt and obvious. Compare, for example, the birthday poems in *The Map of Love* and in this volume. In the earlier poem:

> Twenty-four years remind the tears of my eyes. . . .

and:

> In the final direction of the elementary town
> I advance for as long as forever is.[27]

In the later one:

> It was my thirtieth year to heaven. . . .

and:

> O may my heart's truth
> Still be sung
> On this high hill in a year's turning.[28]

The differences do not indicate so much that Thomas has changed as that he has developed. A similar development is observable in the revision of "Unluckily for a Death," which was originally called "Poem (To Caitlin)," was sent to Vernon Watkins in (probably) May 1939, first published in *Life and Letters Today* in October of the same year, and then in a considerably revised form in *Deaths and Entrances*. As Watkins says, "all the changes made in its rewriting were movements away from ironical, and towards religious statement."[29] In the version sent to Vernon Watkins, the poem ends:

> Though the puffed phoenix stir in the rocks
> And lucklessly fair or sycorax the widow wait,
> We abide with our pride, the unalterable light,
> On this turning lump of mistakes.

The final version reads:

> O my true love, hold me.
> In your every inch and glance is the globe of genesis spun,
> And the living earth your sons.[30]

The most obviously religious of the poems in *Deaths and Entrances* are "A Refusal to Mourn," "Ceremony after a Fire Raid," "Vision and Prayer," and "Fern Hill," but the religious impulse informs almost every poem in the volume. "Fern Hill" is one of the best-known and best-loved of Thomas's poems. It has been perhaps too easy for critics to point out that this poem, even more than the "Poem in October," has "in a more contemporary idiom, without the framework of a theology and a conventional terminology ... the same visionary splendour and the same rapturous illumination ... ," as *Centuries of Meditation*.[31] But to say that "Fern Hill" reminds us of Vaughan and Traherne is to make only a partial appreciation of the poem. One of its most striking features, and one which differentiates it from those passages in Vaughan and Traherne to which it has been so often compared, is that obsession with Time, which D. C. Muecke noted as recurrent in Thomas's work as a whole:

Time let me hail and climb
Golden in the heydays of his eyes. . . .

And once below a time I lordly had the trees and
    leaves
    Trail with daisies and barley
Down the rivers of the windfall light. . . .

Time let me play and be
Golden in the mercy of his means. . . .

And nothing I cared, at my sky blue trades, that time
    allows
In all his tuneful turning so few and such morning
    songs
        Before the children green and golden
        Follow him out of grace. . . .

Time held me green and dying
Though I sang in my chains like the sea. . . .[32]

This insistent repetition in the poem of the word "Time,"
of the concept of time, of the "Time passes" which is one
of the structural motifs of *Under Milk Wood*, makes us
become aware of how many other phrases in the poem
are also loaded with the same intimations of temporality,
and therefore, since this is a poem about a human being
(the poet himself without disguise or *persona*), of mortality
as well:

Now as I *was* young and easy. . . .

I *was* prince of the apple towns. . . .

And as I *was* green and carefree. . . .

. . . it *was* running, it *was* lovely. . . .

. . . it *was* all shining. . . .

I *ran* my heedless ways. . . .

We might describe this poem by saying that in it Thomas is celebrating what Robert Graves called

> the greatness, rareness, muchness,
> Fewness of this precious only
> Endless world . . .[33]

celebrating it by an act of deliberate and almost total recall, saying in effect, "This, as I remember it, was what it was like to be a child." And the loveliness and happiness that he recalls and celebrates are poignantly enhanced by the undertone of the *tempus fugit* theme which runs through the poem, and with which it ends:

> Time held me green and dying
> Though I sang in my chains like the sea.[34]

To say so much is to describe the poem, to reduce it to some such statement as "Duw, man, the world was a wonderful place when I was a child. But, alas, Time passes." Paraphrasably, the poem is trite enough: the critical question is, how does Thomas convince us of the authenticity and significance of his vision of childhood? He does so, first of all, by the concrete quality of the child's world that he recalls and displays to us. That world, as befits a child's world, is full of actual, visible, tangible objects: apple boughs, house, grass, the dingle, wagons, trees, leaves, daisies, barley, barns, the yard, the farm, the sun, the calves, the foxes, the pebbles, the streams, the hayfields, chimneys, the dew, the cock, the sky, the fields, pheasants, clouds, hay, the swallow-thronged loft. This is indeed a rich, full world, crammed with things, and all sharply and colourfully realised. But it is not merely a catalogue or inventory of the farm that Thomas gives us. The objects are mentioned casually and in different ways, literally and metaphorically, so that it is only when we examine the poem closely that we realise how many of them there are. The long, flowing rhythms, the piled-up sentences and the frequent use of the word "and," combine to give a suggestion of the breathless incoherence of a child recounting the glory and wonder of a day: "And I climbed the appletrees, and there were horses, and at night I could hear the owls, and, and, and . . .". In both of these ways, then—in the presented wealth of concrete objects, and in the suggestion that it is actually a child speaking—the poem induces in us, without our necessarily being aware of the fact as we read, a willingness to believe what the poem is saying.

Again, in harmony with its evocation of childhood, the poem employs an extremely simple vocabulary; there is in it not a single "difficult" or unusual word. Similarly, though the sentences are long, their construction is extremely simple: it is that primitive, accumulative construction which is common in the speech of children. On the other hand, one of the striking features of the poem is the richness, unusualness, and vividness of its imagery. But although they are striking and unusual, the images too are really very simple—no jarring note of intellectual or emotional complexity is struck by any of them. In fact, children, who do not make the rigid adult distinction between the literal and the metaphorical, accept the images of this poem quite happily and do not find anything strange in them.

Thomas employs here four overlapping kinds of imagery. There is the kind of image he had made peculiarly his own, consisting of a familiar phrase given a surprising twist: "happy as the grass was green," "once below a time" (which he had already used as the first line and title of a poem omitted from *Deaths and Entrances* but reinstated in *Collected Poems*), "all the sun running." There are comparisons, implicit or explicit, which would occur naturally to a child: "I was huntsman and herdsman, the calves | Sang to my horn", "the hay | Fields high as the house." There is the use again of the childlike idea he had employed in "The Hunchback in the Park," the

concept of the farm going away at night and returning in
the morning when the child awakes:

> And nightly under the simple stars
> As I rode to sleep the owls were bearing the farm
> away, . . .

> And then to awake, and the farm, like a wanderer
> white
> With the dew, come back, the cock on his shoulder.[35]

And finally there is the chapel imagery, reminiscently
Biblical, which is to be found throughout Thomas's
poetry: "And the sabbath rang slowly | In the pebbles of
the holy streams," "it was Adam and maiden."

The first of these kinds of imagery has received some
critical attention. Geoffrey Grigson, in a notorious
attack, says that what he calls "the cliché turned" is
"word-tumbling without either gravity of point, or point
of fun. . . ."[36] In fact, Thomas uses this device compara-
tively rarely, and always with point. The phrase "happy
as the grass was green," for example, is a beautifully
concise way of conveying two notions, that of the un-
blemished happiness of childhood and that of the child's
vivid impression of external nature. Similarly, the phrase
"a bad coin in your socket" from an earlier poem ("To
Others than You") is apt and precise. The poem, which
begins with an isolated line, "Friend by enemy I call you
out," is, as Fraser says, one "which warns us wholesomely
against the kind of undue familiarity to which his public
legend, the memory of his personality, the critic's dan-
gerous passion for summary judgements, might all invite
us."[37] Into this transformed cliché Thomas compressed
three ideas: "coin in a pocket" refers to money and the
"friendship" it can buy; "a bad coin" refers to the
familiar expression "turning up like a bad penny," which
was something Thomas did, and knew he did, to friends
who had money; and "coin in a socket" refers to the

custom of putting pennies on the eyes of the dead, and so
to the death which such false friendship as the poem is
about represents. Such subdued punning is apparent
elsewhere in single words in Thomas's poems. In "Once
it was the Colour of Saying" there is a "capsized field
where a school sat still." The field is "capsized" because
it is on a hillside and looks upset or overturned and also
because the distance from which it is seen reduces it to
the size of a schoolboy's cap. More subtly, in "Over Sir
John's Hill," we have

> And I who hear the tune of the slow,
> Wear-willow river.[38]

The river is "wear-willow" both because it wears the
willow as clothing or ornament and because it wears the
willow away.

Deaths and Entrances also contained the three longest
poems (apart from the sonnet sequence) that Thomas
had written so far: "A Winter's Tale," "Vision and
Prayer," and "Ballad of the Long-legged Bait." As
Linden Huddlestone pointed out,[39] "A Winter's Tale" is
a recension of ll. 3–12 of the first poem in *The Map of Love*,
"Because the Pleasure-Bird Whistles." The important
word in the title is "tale"—the poem, this word an-
nounces, is to be the telling of a legendary story, of something that happened long ago, once upon or below a time.
We should no more expect to be able to pin this down to
any one specific meaning than we can any other fairy-
tale. We can, however, say that it has certain references—
to love, to death.

We can, indeed, go further, and agree with Huddlestone that the poem may be interpreted on three different
levels (which are not necessarily exclusive of each other).
We may read the poem, as I have already suggested, as a
"love story of magic fairy-tale character," and on this
level it has certain affinities with episodes in various
mythologies. Or, secondly, we may read it as an allegory

F

of profane love, of romantic passion. The protagonist of
the poem, the man

> Torn and alone in a farm house in a fold
> Of fields . . .
> By the spit and the black pot in the log bright light . . .

> At the point of love, forsaken and afraid[40]

—this man is, at the beginning of the poem, in the usual
position of the romantic lover, separate from his love or
not yet having found her. At the end of the poem his
desire ("Christ! that my love were in my arms") has
been granted; and the poem is, though it purports to be a
narrative, rather a celebration of this finding of "the
right true end" of love. Or, thirdly, we may read the
poem as an allegory of sacred love. For such a reading,
analogies may be found in the poems of Richard Crashaw
and St John of the Cross.

"A Winter's Tale" is one of Thomas's greatest technical
triumphs—the whole poem moves with a superb assurance; the sense of strain apparent in some of his poems is
completely lacking here. The poem begins with a beautifully exact evocation of what a British White Christmas is
traditionally supposed to be like—the properties are those
of a Christmas card (before Christmas cards became
sophisticated), but the words and the images are inter-
woven in such a way as to give a complete visual and
tactile impression of whiteness, cold, and stillness: "the
snow blind twilight," "floating fields from the farm in the
cup of the vales," "The pale breath of cattle," "And
the stars falling cold, | And the smell of hay in the snow,"
"and the frozen hold | Flocked with the sheep-white smoke
of the farm house cowl." The whole poem turns on the
repetition of the words "Listen" and "Look":

> Listen. The minstrels sing
> In the departed villages. . . .

Time sings through the intricately dead snow drop.
  Listen. . . .

  Look. And the dancers move
On the departed, snow bushed green, wanton in
  moon light
As a dust of pigeons. . . .

For love, the long ago she bird rises. Look.[41]

(Thomas was to use the same simple but effective device
later in *Under Milk Wood*.) The repetition of these elemen-
tary and commanding words in the middle of the poem is
not a mere verbalism; rather it is an example of what
R. P. Blackmur has characterised as "language as
gesture." "Language," says Mr Blackmur, "is made of
words, and gesture is made of motion. . . . Words are
made of motion, made of action or response, at whatever
remove; and gesture is made of language—made of the
language beneath or beyond or alongside of the language
of words."[42] This "Listen" and this "Look" of Thomas's
are imperative and in no way cheating gestures, since the
poet proceeds to give us something to listen to and to look
at; and since these words are the hinges on which the
poem turns.

Huddlestone characterised the poem as having "coherence of imagery, validity of symbols, and a balance of
reason, emotion, and imagination." Even more pertinently, W. S. Merwin, in an interesting essay on Thomas
called "The Religious Poet," said that in this poem "the
fact has made myth." Although he does not use the term,
Merwin does in effect demonstrate that "A Winter's
Tale" is a "White Goddess" poem, whether Thomas invented or remembered the midwinter and rebirth myth
which is its narrative core.

He has 'made' the myth whether or not he invented the
skeletal story, for it is his own imagination which has

given it its immediacy and power, which has seen love-in-death, the 'she bird', with such certainty as heavenly and all-powerful, which has made articulate within the metaphor itself the triumph of the rite which is life.[43]

"Vision and Prayer" is exactly what the title says it is. In the first part of the poem we have Thomas's vision of the divinity of man and of the reality of divine love:

> And upright Adam
> Sang upon origin!
> . . . the happening
> Of saints to their vision![44]

In the second part we have Thomas's prayer for the truth of resurrection:

> I pray
> May the crimson
> Sun spin a grave grey
> And the colour of clay
> Stream upon his martyrdom
> In the interpreted evening
> And the known dark of the earth amen.[45]

In the sonnet-sequence of *Twenty-five Poems*, Thomas had presented a movement from a despair that might be characterised as pagan, through a new-born hope consequent upon the crucifixion, to the renewal of hope in the promise of resurrection. "Vision and Prayer" shows a development of Thomas's religious imagination. The poem is too contrived to be among Thomas's best (the shape of the two parts on the printed page depends too much on typographical assistance, and perhaps owes as much to the example of E. E. Cummings—a poet Thomas greatly admired—as to that of George Herbert). But the dominant note of the whole poem is again of celebration and exultation, the "Cry Joy" of the earlier "A Saint about to Fall":

> I pray though I belong
> Not wholly to that lamenting
> Brethren for joy has moved within
> The inmost marrow of my heart bone.[46]

W. Y. Tindall tells us that "one day in a bar on West 23rd Street," Dylan Thomas explicated the central meaning of "Ballad of the Long-legged Bait" thus: "a young man goes out to fish for sexual experience, but he catches a family, the church, and the village green. Indeed, he himself is caught by his bait."[47] The general direction of the "Ballad of the Long-legged Bait" is clear enough, and the poem contains some of Thomas's most dazzling lines, though details remain obscure even after repeated readings. At the same time, we must recognise that Thomas's statement of his intention by no means exhausts the meaning of the poem. Elder Olson has suggested that the theme of the poem is the idea of winning salvation through the mortification of the flesh; and if we take mortification, somewhat loosely, to mean the progress from adolescence to manhood, we can agree with this reading. (One of the most revealing anecdotes in Brinnin's book on Thomas in America tells how Thomas in a New York bar said about a young couple in a booth, "their heads amorously together": "How filthy!" Accused of being a Puritan, the poet said "I *am* a Puritan"—there was nothing else he could have been or said.) Even more important than Thomas's stated intention is the fact that, in Olson's words, "the theme of the whole poem is given the emotional power of its legend."[48]

> Sails drank the wind, and white as milk
> He sped into the drinking dark;
> The sun shipwrecked west on a pearl
> And the moon swam out of its hulk. . . .

Round her trailed wrist fresh water weaves;
With moving fish and rounded stones
Up and down the greater waves
A separate river breathes and runs; . . .

. . . nothing remains
Of the pacing, famous sea but its speech, . . .

He stands alone at the door of his house,
With his long-legged heart in his hand.[49]

Thomas's statement (and who knows how serious it was?)
may be taken as the beginning of an explanation of the
poem: its "legend" is obviously Biblical. As Olson
noticed, the book of the Bible that informs the "Ballad" is
one that has notably haunted the Welsh nonconformist
imagination, the book of Revelation; and in particular
these two verses:

And the sea gave up the dead which were in it; and
death and hell delivered up the dead which were in
them: and they were judged every man according to
their works.[50]

and:

And I saw a new heaven and a new earth: for the first
heaven and the first earth were passed away; and
there was no more sea.[51]

Thomas's poem transmutes these tremendous and
agonised statements into:

And through the sundered water crawls
A garden holding to her hand
With birds and animals

With men and women and waterfalls[52]

and

There is nothing left of the sea but its sound
Under the earth the loud sea walks,
In deathbeds of orchards the boat dies down
And the bait is drowned among hayricks.[53]

I am diffident about accepting Fraser's restatement of Olson's interpretation of the poem as "a kind of small allegory about the struggle inside Thomas, a typically Welsh struggle, between natural sensuality and puritan mysticism."[54] But even such a formulation is closer to the poem than the derivation, indulged in by some critics, from Rimbaud's "Le Bateau ivre." (The title itself is much more likely to be derived from Yeats than from Rimbaud.) The poem does not come off in the way "A Winter's Tale" comes off, but it is a haunting and powerful poem nevertheless, one in which, as Olson says, "the salvation takes on the beauty and mystery of the resurrection of the dead and the past from the sea":

Strike and sing his catch of fields
For the surge is sown with barley,
The cattle graze on the covered foam,
The hills have footed the waves away,

With wild sea fillies and soaking bridles
With salty colts and gales in their limbs
All the horses of his haul of miracles
Gallop through the arched, green farms. . . .

And the streets that the fisherman combed
When his long-legged flesh was a wind on fire
And his loin was a hunting flame

Coil from the thoroughfares of her hair
And terribly lead him home alive
Lead her prodigal home to his terror,
The furious ox-killing house of love.[55]

REFERENCES

1. Karl Shapiro, "Dylan Thomas," in Tedlock, p. 272.
2. *Letters*, p. 70.
3. *Letters*, p. 19.
4. Rayner Heppenstall, *Four Absentees*, London 1960, pp. 149–50.
5. In *New World Writing, Seventh Mentor Selection*, New York 1955, pp. 134–5.
6. *Q.E.O.M.*, p. 92.
7. *Q.E.O.M.*, p. 53.
8. *Letters*, p. 111.
9. *New World Writing*, p. 138.
10. *Letters*, p. 20.
11. D. C. Muecke, " 'Come back! Come back!', A Theme in Dylan Thomas's Prose," in *Meanjin*, xviii (1959), 69–76.
12. *C.P.*, p. 173.
13. *Adventures*, pp. 13–14.
14. Olson, *The Poetry of Dylan Thomas*, p. 23.
15. *C.P.*, p. 135.
16. Olson, *The Poetry of Dylan Thomas*, p. 22.
17. Olson, *op. cit.*, pp. 23.
18. *C.P.*, p. 101.
19. *Q.E.O.M.*, pp. 2, 10.
20. *C.P.*, p. 111.
21. Treece, *Dylan Thomas*, London 1949, pp. 47–8.
22. Brinnin, *Dylan Thomas in America*, pp. 103–4.
23. *Letters*, p. 17.
24. Treece, *Dylan Thomas*, London 1949, pp. 46–7.
25. *C.P.*, p. 170.
26. Cid Corman, "Dylan Thomas: Rhetorician in Mid-Career," in Tedlock, p. 225.
27. *C.P.*, p. 99.
28. *C.P.*, pp. 102–4.
29. *Letters*, p. 64.
30. *C.P.*, p. 110.
31. E. Glyn Lewis, "Dylan Thomas," in the *Welsh Review*, vii (1948), pp. 276–7.
32. *C.P.*, pp. 159–61.
33. Robert Graves, "Warning to Children," in his *Collected Poems 1959*, p. 46.
34. *C.P.*, p. 161.
35. *C.P.*, p. 160.
36. Geoffrey Grigson, "How much me now your Acrobatics Amaze," in Tedlock, p. 163.
37. G. S. Fraser, *Dylan Thomas*, p. 34.
38. *C.P.*, p. 169.
39. Linden Huddlestone, "An Approach to Dylan Thomas," in *Penguin New Writing*, 35 (1948), p. 152.
40. *C.P.*, pp. 119–20.
41. *C.P.*, p. 121.
42. R. P. Blackmur, *Language as Gesture*, London 1954, p. 3.
43. W. S. Merwin, "The Religious Poet," in Tedlock, p. 245.
44. *C.P.*, p. 142.
45. *C.P.*, p. 147.
46. *C.P.*, p. 143.
47. W. Y. Tindall, *The Literary Symbol*, Bloomington, Indiana, 1955, p. 155.

48. Olson, *The Poetry of Dylan Thomas*, p. 25.

49. *C.P.*, pp. 149, 156, 157.

50. Rev. xx. 13.

51. Rev. xxi. 1.

52. *C.P.*, p. 155.

53. *C.P.*, p. 157.

54. Fraser, *Dylan Thomas*, p. 31.

55. *C.P.*, pp. 156, 157.

CHAPTER IV

AMERICA AND COUNTRY HEAVEN

After the War, the Thomases moved back to Oxfordshire for a while. In 1947 the poet left the shores of Britain for the first time on a visit to Italy. In 1948 he moved to the most pleasing and, paradoxically in the light of the short (he would have added good) time he was actually there, the most permanent of his many homes after 5 Cwmdonkin Drive. This was the Boat House in Laugharne—

> my seashaken house
> On a breakneck of rocks
> Tangled with chirrup and fruit,
> Froth, flute, fin and quill
> At a wood's dancing hoof.[1]

For some years, aware of his responsibilities as a married man and the father of a family, and equally aware of his own inability or unwillingness to discharge those responsibilities in any ordinary way, conscious, in other words, that he could only make money to live on and, more important, for his family to live on, through his poetry and his public personality, Thomas had been contemplating with a sort of horrified fascination the prospect of lecturing and reading poetry in America. As early as 1945 we find him writing about the possibilities to Oscar Williams, who had been responsible for many of his American publications. With his customary wry self-depreciation he listed his qualifications:

I can read aloud, through sonorous asthma, with pomp; I can lecture on the trend of Y, or X at the crossroads, or Z: whither? with an assurance whose shiftiness can be seen only from the front row; I can write script and radio films [*sic*], of a sort; I can—and so on with the list that could be, and is, supplied by every person fit for nothing but his shameful ability to fit into the hack ends of commercial, intellectual, or personal, advertisement.[2]

Meanwhile, in America itself, Brinnin had been for some years unsuccessfully trying to engineer an American visit by the Welsh poet. When in 1949 Brinnin became director of the Poetry Center of the Young Men's and Women's Hebrew Association in New York, he was able to invite Thomas directly himself. After checking on Brinnin with his American publisher, James Laughlin of New Directions, Thomas warmly accepted the offer, and on 21 Feb. 1950 landed in America for the first time.

On one level, the story of the last three years of Thomas's life has been told in Brinnin's sad, disquieting book, *Dylan Thomas in America*. The book unfortunately has its value as a record of those years and of the poet's American experience. Regarded as a complete account, it suffers from two serious omissions. One of these is bravely expressed by Caitlin Thomas in her preliminary statement to the book:

> There is no such thing as the one true Dylan Thomas. . . . I want only to make clear that an intensive handful of months, at divided intervals, over a comparatively short number of years do not, however accurately recorded and with whatever honest intentions, do justice to the circumference of the subject.[3]

Since the book purports to be no more than an account of Dylan Thomas in America (it could be more accurately described as an account of Brinnin's experience of Thomas), the other omission from it is any consideration, other than incidentally, of what Thomas wrote during those years.

At the expense of chronology, it is convenient to discuss Thomas's broadcast scripts and *The Doctor and the Devils* along with *Under Milk Wood*. Although he never belonged to the B.B.C. staff and always refused regular commitments, Thomas's work and reputation in sound-broadcasting were triple: as radio actor, as verse-reader, and as writer of his own scripts. As a radio actor he was versatile and memorable, and he could obviously have made a professional living at this work. (As a schoolboy and young man in Swansea he had done a great deal of acting.) As a verse-reader he was unique in the combination of his resonant, but flexible, voice and the subtle understanding of the poems he read. He was fond of referring to his style of reading as "booming," and was very well aware of its dangers:

For what a reader-aloud of his own poems so often does, is to mawken or melodramatize them, making a single simple phrase break with the fears or throb with the terrors from which he deludes himself the phrase has been born.[4]

Thomas avoided the dangers because, as his producers, Aneirin Talfan Davies, Roy Campbell, and John Arlott have testified, he approached his readings in a completely professional manner and worked as hard at them as he did at his writing.

His radio scripts (apart from the separately published *Under Milk Wood*) were collected and published in 1954 by Aneirin Talfan Davies under the title *Quite Early one Morning*. Davies divides them into two kinds, roughly "creative" and "more didactic." All of the scripts evince again the care and industry that Thomas put into his work; there is nothing casual or improvised about even the slightest of them. Aneirin Talfan Davies records how the brief script describing the International Eisteddfod at Llangollen was composed:

The week was spent in apparently aimless meandering through the crowded streets of the town, occasional half-hours in the Eisteddfod marquee, and many hours standing at bars of the far from few pubs of the town. Now and then, while standing at the bar, Thomas would tear open an empty cigarette carton, take out a stub of pencil from his pocket, and behind the shelter of a friendly pint he would scribble a few words, sometimes just a single word, and deposit it in the depths of his capacious coat pocket. By the end of the week he had a harvest of these scribbled phrases.

Back at home he spent two days writing up these notes; when he arrived at the studio about an hour before the broadcast, the script was found to be about three minutes short, "but there was no question of adding to it; and there was to be no hurried scribbling in the studio."[5]

One of the most striking devices in these broadcasts is that of the catalogue (akin to, though probably not derived from, the Welsh "dyfalu") a pell-mell piling-up of words and puns and conceits, that at first sounds merely arbitrary, though inspection reveals that all is carefully chosen and ordered. He gives us, for example, the landladies of New Quay, "a cliff-perched town at the far end of Wales":

Landladies, shawled and bloused and aproned with sleep in the curtained, bombasined black of their once spare rooms, remember their loves, their bills, their visitors—dead, decamped, or buried in English deserts till the trumpet of next expensive August roused them again to the world of holiday rain, dismal cliff and sand seen through the weeping windows of front parlours, tasselled table-cloths, stuffed pheasants, ferns in pots, fading photographs of the bearded and censorious dead, autograph albums with a lock of limp and colourless beribboned hair lolling out between the thick black boards.[6]

In these catalogues and elsewhere we notice again and again that reporter's eye for the telling detail that served Thomas well in all his prose:

> the street near Waterloo station where a small boy, wearing cut-down khaki and a steel helmet, pushed a pram full of firewood and shouted, in a dispassionate voice, after each passer-by: 'Where's your tail?'[7]

In America, Brinnin was struck by Thomas's powers of observation, by the way in which, sober or not sober, he noted everything in detail.[8]

But the most interesting feature of the broadcast scripts is the one pointed out by their editor: that, read chronologically, they show a distinct development in Thomas's radio technique, and particularly a development in the direction of a genuine and original radio drama. This development can be clearly traced from "Quite Early one Morning," through "Return Journey," to its culmination in *Under Milk Wood*. In "Quite Early one Morning" we have, among other anticipations of *Under Milk Wood*, the imagined voices of people other than the speaker:

> Clara Tawe Jenkins, 'Madam' they call me,
> An old contralto with her dressing-gown on,
> And I sit at the window and I sing to the sea,
> For the sea does not notice that my voice has gone.[9]

In this piece the voices are only heard, dreamed, or imagined by the poet as he walks through the town of New Quay "Quite early one morning in the winter in Wales." In "Holiday Memory" Thomas approaches more closely to the dramatic in the use of a kind of stichomythia which he was to employ effectively in the later "Play for Voices":

> 'Uncle Owen says he can't find the bottle-opener . . .'
> 'Has he looked under the hall-stand?'
> 'Willy's cut his finger . . .'

'Got your spade?'

'If somebody doesn't kill that dog . . .'

'Uncle Owen says why should the bottle-opener be under the hall-stand?'

'Never again, never again . . .'[10]

"Return Journey" approaches still more closely to the dramatic. The liveliness of the language in this talks-feature, the vividness of the images, the power of Thomas's evocation, are apt to hide from us that the script's greatest virtue lies in its construction. It begins conventionally enough with a narrator, Thomas himself back after an absence of fourteen years in a Swansea changed almost out of recognition by the air-raids. The narrator's account of what he did and what he said is modulated into the voices of other people, but these are dramatically realised, not dreamed or imagined as the voices were in "Quite Early one Morning." First, we have the barmaid and the customers in the hotel, then the old and young reporters, a passer-by, the schoolmaster, the Promenade-man, and the girls of long ago, anonymous voices, and finally the park-keeper. Thomas's return journey has been in search of the young man and the boy he once was, and it ends with the park-keeper's response to his question " 'What has become of him now?' ": the reiteration of the word "Dead."

Of the work that he did in films, Thomas gives us the usual depreciatory account. Sending Oscar Williams some poems from Wales in 1945, he commented:

The longish one, I'm glad to say, has taken a great deal of time and trouble, and has prevented me from writing filmscripts on Rehabilitation, Better Housing, Post War Full Employment, etc, for the socialist film department of the Ministry of Information.[11]

Paradoxically, the only published film-script by Thomas is one of a film that was never made. This is *The*

Doctor and the Devils, based on a story by Donald Taylor
about Burke and Hare, the notorious body-snatchers and
murderers of nineteenth-century Edinburgh. Derek Stanford has adversely criticised this work on the grounds that
it is not sufficiently dramatic, that the intended struggle
of conscience on the question of ends and means is not in
fact embodied in Dr Rock, and that "the figure of the
Doctor remains something of a Byronic 'dummy' for all
the energy of rhetoric which he tries to pump into him."[12]
There is some justification in these strictures, but Stanford
overstates his case. In talking about the work as if it were
a novel or a play, he forgets the important fact that a
film-script, even by a man of Thomas's genius, is only one
contribution to the composite which is a film. Reviewing
the book in *Poetry* (Chicago), the American critic, Parker
Tyler, was much nearer the mark when he characterised
it as "a remarkably competent and vivid melodrama
which its scriptist does not uproot from the conven-
tion in which its inventor, Donald Taylor, embedded
it. . . ."[13]

What is most striking about *The Doctor and the Devils* is
its readability, the spendthrift way in which Thomas
lavishes words and images on something that normally
would not have been published at all. He evokes the
nineteenth-century Edinburgh scene for us as vividly as
ever his own Laugharne or Swansea:

The straw-strewn cobbles of the Market are crowded
with stalls. Stalls that sell rags and bones, kept by rags
and bones. Stalls that sell odds and ends of every odd
kind, odd boots, bits of old meat, fish heads, trinkets,
hats with feathers, broad-sheets, hammers. Stalls with
shawls. Stalls like ash bins. Anything that is marketable,
to the very poor.[14]

Thomas compresses a world of information and suggestion into a single, flashing phrase:

There are many, many children, some very old.[15]

Then sudden light, and Fallon's hands, palms down-
wards, fingers stretched and tautened, murdering
down the screen.[16]

And there is the macabre, Dickensian humour of the
depiction of the two murderers and their activities:

BROOM: Hammer him in, hammer him in. Four pounds
    rent all dead in a box.
FALLON: Now who would've thought old Daniel could
    be so mean. Dying without a word, and owing us
    four pounds. He didn't even have a penny piece
    hidden under the straw . . .
BROOM: If only he was alive again so that I could kill
    him with my hands . . .
FALLON: And all he left was a bit of a broken pipe . . .
    And livin' here all these months on the fat of the
    land . . . Many's the night I've beaten the rats off
    him myself. . . .[17]

It is in this realisation of character and background
atmosphere that *The Doctor and the Devils* is most powerful.
  This film-script and many of the radio-scripts may be
regarded as preliminary exercises for Thomas's most
widely-known work, the "Play for Voices," *Under Milk
Wood*. The origin of this goes back to 1939. Richard
Hughes says:

The real genesis of UNDER MILKWOOD was an amateur
dramatic performance of some rubbishy play in the
Laugharne 'Memorial Hall' in the autumn of 1939.
Dylan, my wife, Mr Gleed the butcher, and I myself
were the cast. Talking it over afterwards Dylan conceived the idea of a play to be written by the two of us
based on actual Laugharne characters, and these people
themselves should play their own parts! They were

G

each and all so convinced (he felt) that their eccentric behaviour was exactly the way to go on that he thought they would be only too glad for a chance to prove it in public![18]

He had actually been asked in the previous year by a producer on the Welsh B.B.C. to write a dramatic feature in verse, and had replied that he doubted his ability to do it, because he wrote so slowly, "and the result, dramatically, is too often like a man shouting under the sea."[19] The idea, however, continued to fascinate him. The story of the gradual evolution of *Under Milk Wood* is told by Daniel Jones in his preface to the published work. Its immediate origin lay in the development of "Quite Early one Morning," which was broadcast in 1945. At first, this was to be combined with the idea of "The Town that was Mad" which Thomas had first propounded to Richard Hughes in 1939. The next stage in its growth is best told in his own words. In October 1951, he sent to Marguerite Caetani, the editor of *Botteghe Oscure*, the manuscript of *Llareggub. A Piece for Radio perhaps*, and in the accompanying letter explained:

I told you, as you may remember, that I was working on a play, mostly in verse. This, I have reluctantly, and, I hope, only temporarily, abandoned: the language was altogether swamping the subject; the comedy, for that was what it was originally intended to be, was lost in the complicated violence of the words: ... But out of my working, however vainly, on it, came the idea of Llareggub. ... Out of it came the idea that I write a piece, a play, an impression for voices, an entertainment out of the darkness, of the town I live in, and to write it simply and warmly and comically with lots of movement and varieties of moods, so that, at many levels, through sight and speech, description and dialogue, evocation and parody, you came to know the town as an inhabitant of it.[20]

These comments by the author provide as good criticism as has been written of *Under Milk Wood*. (Thomas eventually changed the title because he felt that the joke in the coined name, Llareggub—which he had first used in his story "The Orchards"—was a small one, and because he feared the name would be forbidding to American audiences.[21] The spelling "Llaregyb" in the published version simply removes the joke and is quite pointless.)

Under Milk Wood is not a play at all in any strict sense of the word. Some critics have found fault with the work for this reason. Derek Stanford says:

> Now if we begin by defining a drama as a form of stage narrative possessed of a *dénouement*, it will be hard to allow that *Under Milk Wood* is a drama at all. . . . The actions . . . are episodic rather than dramatic . . . the characters . . . are static unephemeral creations.[22]

More recently, David Holbrook has stated:

> There is nothing essentially dramatic about the work, because the embodiments have no moral existences, and there is no conflict, development, or synthesis: everything is equally of amusing interest, as to a child, and this lack of essential drama makes *Under Milk Wood* a tedious piece of verbal 'ingenuity', 'redeemed' only by its innuendoes and salacious jokes.[23]

Such criticism misses the point. *Under Milk Wood* was not intended to be dramatic: it is exactly what Thomas himself called it, "an impression for voices, an entertainment out of the darkness, of the town I live in." But Thomas has moved a long way from the merely impressionistic evocation of a small Welsh seaside town that he had given in "Quite Early one Morning." There, the poet walking through the town in the morning had wondered

What big seas of dreams ran in the Captain's sleep?
Over what blue-whaled waves did he sail through a

rainbow hail of flying fishes to the music of Circe's swinish island?[24]

Now he gives us blind Captain Cat himself, dreaming, and awake:

> I'll tell you no lies.
> The only sea I saw
> Was the seesaw sea
> With you riding on it.
> Lie down, lie easy.
> Let me shipwreck in your thighs.[25]

and:

All the women are out this morning, in the sun. You can tell it's Spring. There goes Mrs Cherry, you can tell her by her trotters, off she trots new as a daisy. Who's that talking by the pump? Mrs Floyd and Boyo, talking flat fish. What can you talk about flat fish?[26]

And in addition to Captain Cat there are all the other odd, innocent, eccentric characters who live in Llareggub, under Milk Wood: Myfanwy Price and Mog Edwards, Mr Waldo, Mrs Ogmore-Pritchard, Organ Morgan, Butcher Beynon, and the rest. If we compare these with the characters in a play proper, we must agree with Holbrook that they show no conflict or development, and with Stanford that there are no conversions and no retrogressions. We go through a whole day in the life of Llareggub, and at the end of it the characters are exactly as they were at the beginning, and nothing at all has happened. But this is precisely Thomas's intention. The characters are admittedly drawn by a caricaturist's rather than a portraitist's hand, but that hand is skilful and incisive. Richard Hughes says that "for anyone who had lived in Laugharne the composite portrait of the place and its people is perfect—and *yet* not a single character in it, individually, is drawn from the life—except perhaps Polly Garter."[27]

No dramatic conflict, no development of character, no action in the usual dramatic sense (though there is a surprising amount of movement, from character to character, from one part of the village to another, from the present to the past and back again)—it is all too easy to list qualities that are missing from *Under Milk Wood* if we insist on regarding it as a play. On the other hand, its virtues are even more obvious: the brilliant use of language and imagery to create atmosphere and character (though this is occasionally overdone), the rollicking sense of humour, the joyful bawdy. The great virtue of the work, however, is none of these, but its informing sense of compassion, a compassion which is extended to all the characters, not merely to such an obviously sympathetic one as Captain Cat. We can see this very clearly in the case of the Reverend Eli Jenkins. (Thomas himself played this part in the first reading of the work in New York.) The first sketch of this character is to be found in "Quite Early one Morning." His clergyman here is pretty obviously derived from the characters of Caradoc Evans's stories (with perhaps a hint from T. F. Powys):

> Parchedig Thomas Evans making morning tea,
> Very weak tea, too, you mustn't waste a leaf.
> Every morning making tea in my house by the sea,
> I am troubled by one thing only, and that, belief.[28]

When Thomas developed this character into the Reverend Eli Jenkins, he still gave us a figure of fun, who "gropes out of bed into his preacher's black, combs back his bard's white hair, forgets to wash, . . . remembers his own verses and tells them softly to empty Coronation Street. . . ." But the fun is very gentle. The verses attributed to him are indeed parodies, but they are parodies so close to the originals (which are still being written by many earnest souls in Wales) that, out of context, one would not guess so.

When the Reverend Eli Jenkins hears Polly Garter's song, and comments "Praise the Lord! We are a musical nation,"[29] the incongruity is not intended to be merely funny. Thomas explained to Marguerite Caetani that he intended the piece to be in two halves: the first half would establish the town and its characters and their behaviours; in the second half "the pieces of the town will fit together; the reasons for all these behaviours (so far but hinted at) will be made apparent." He had intended to have two predominant voices, that of the preacher, and that of the "anonymous exhibitor and chronicler" or First Voice. He summed up his intentions when he said that Mary Ann Sailors, who believes the town is the chosen land, "is not at all mad: she merely believes in heaven on earth. And so with all of them, all the eccentrics whose eccentricities, in these first pages, are but briefly and impressionistically noted: all, by their own rights, are ordinary and good: and the 1st Voice, and the poet preacher, never judge nor condemn but explain and make strangely simple and simply strange."[30]

Thomas finished the first version of the work, writing very much against time, for a reading in New York. Before leaving for America on his last trip, he completed an extended version for broadcasting at the request of the B.B.C., but he died before making a final revision. Some of the weaknesses in the play's structure—especially a certain lack of balance between the two parts—can obviously be attributed to this fact. As it stands, however, the work is near enough to completion; and we can see that the innocent and unjudging Reverend Eli Jenkins is a focal point, as well as being the character who most fully embodies Dylan Thomas's own attitude to the inhabitants of Llareggub.

The Reverend Eli is humble: "I know there are | Towns lovelier than ours, | . . . And sweeter bards than I to sing"; and he is all-compassionate: "O please to keep Thy lovely eye | On all poor creatures born to die."[31] In his goodness and his innocence he loves everybody. The Reverend Eli therefore provides, in fact, as does Captain Cat in a different way (the ways are not so opposed as they might be taken to be) that "moral placing" which David Holbrook finds missing from the work.[32] *Under Milk Wood* is really a set of variations on the theme of love. This is obvious enough in the cases of Captain Cat remembering Rosie Probert, Polly Garter with her babies, Sinbad Sailors yearning for Gossamer Beynon, Gossamer herself twitching with Spring, Mae Rose Cottage wanting to grow up and sin. It is also true of Dai Bread and his two wives, and of Mrs Cherry Owen who has two husbands in the one person, one sober by day and one drunk by night. But it is true as well of Myfanwy Price and Mog Edwards, who love each other but will never marry, of Mrs Ogmore-Pritchard and the two ghosts in her immaculate house, of Mr and Mrs Pugh so indispensable to each other for her nagging and his plotting.

In *The Doctor and the Devils*, more convincingly than in the often contrived diabolism of *The Map of Love*, Thomas had shown that he was capable of a very thorough and frightening representation of evil, both the subhuman and wholly degraded evil that is the product of hopeless destitution and the more subtle evil of the high-minded but intellectually arrogant man who persuades himself that the ends justify the means. In *Under Milk Wood* he does something that is incomparably more difficult: he presents us with a vision of a world that is completely good, where there is no evil and no sin, and yet is a world very human, very fallible, and extremely interesting both to its inhabitants and to us.

This vision of goodness, innocence, and happiness is also to be found in the last poems that he wrote. When the *Collected Poems* appeared in 1952, several critics pointed out, in tones ranging from triumphant vituperation to sorrowful admission, that the volume contained only six poems written since the publication of *Deaths and*

Entrances in 1946. The observation has been repeated since Thomas's death, and usually accompanied by the assertion that his poetic powers were failing. In a way, this forms part of the unfortunate Dylan Legend. As a very young man in London, he had been fond of announcing that he had but a short time left to live, and there were always people gullible enough to believe him. As he went on living and his fame increased, the envious could always derive some satisfaction from predicting his imminent death or, failing that, the drying up of his talents. Nothing that Thomas did or said in his last years discouraged these prophets of gloom and disaster. But it is hard now to see any real justification for the charge that Thomas's powers were in any way failing. Admittedly, he wrote little poetry between 1946 and 1953; but the major part of that limited output ("In Country Sleep," "Over Sir John's Hill," and "In the white Giant's Thigh," which were part of an intended long poem) was on a bigger scale than anything he had planned before except, possibly, the abandoned sonnet-sequence. And the last years of his life were the most frantic ones that he spent. Sick, perpetually harassed by debt and problems he could not deal with, he still managed to write *The Doctor and the Devils* and *Under Milk Wood* and make the four American tours which, while they brought him greater fame than ever, undoubtedly also took an incalculable toll of his mental and physical resources.

It may be true, though it must remain hypothetical (and there is no evidence for it in the last poems themselves), that Thomas had reached the end of a stage of his development as a poet. He seems to have felt this quite seriously himself. He told Daniel Jones that, after the publication of *Collected Poems*, "he intended to turn from the strictly personal kind of poetry to a more public form of expression, and to large-scale dramatic works in particular, where there would be scope for all his versatility, for his gifts of humour and characterisation as well as his genius for poetry."[33] Similarly, another friend, Philip Burton, records that when he saw Thomas a few days before the latter flew to America for his last trip, the poet discussed with him, at length and in detail, not only *Under Milk Wood* which he had just finished for the B.B.C., but also the opera-libretto he was going to write (at Aldous Huxley's suggestion) for Igor Stravinsky, and a play which he envisaged as being more properly dramatic than his piece for radio.[34]

The poems themselves of these last years of his life ("Do not go Gentle into that Good Night," the last five poems in *Collected Poems*, the "Author's Prologue" to that volume, and the unfinished "Elegy" to his father) certainly show no signs of failing powers. Thomas was writing fewer poems than when he had been the marvellous boy just up from Swansea, but they were bigger poems. The slightest of these poems is the piece of lyrical bawdy entitled "Lament" (which I was once not allowed to read on the B.B.C. European Service). This account of a rake's progress until "my soul found a sunday wife . . . And all the deadly virtues plague my death!", though it has no doubt some connexions with aspects of the poet's own life and more with the roaring boy of the legend, is chiefly remarkable for its objectivity and its craftsmanship. The "I" of this poem is neither Dylan Thomas himself nor a *persona*, but an objectively realised character.

The three poems, "In Country Sleep," "Over Sir John's Hill," and "In the white Giant's Thigh", were parts of a projected long poem on an ambitious scale. When he broadcast the three poems on the B.B.C. Third Programme in 1950 Thomas said of his long poem "in preparation":

The poem is to be called 'In Country Heaven'. The godhead, the author, the milky-way farmer, the first cause, architect, lamplighter, quintessence, the beginning Word, the anthropomorphic bowler-out and blackballer, the stuff of all men, scapegoat, martyr, maker, woe-bearer—He, on top of a hill in heaven, weeps whenever, outside that state of being called his country, one of his worlds drops dead, vanishes screaming, shrivels, explodes, murders itself. And, when he weeps, Light and his tears glide down together, hand in hand. So, at the beginning of the projected poem, he weeps, and Country Heaven is suddenly dark. Bushes and owls blow out like candles. And the countrymen of heaven crouch all together under the hedges and, among themselves in the tear-salt darkness, surmise which world, which star, which of their late, turning homes, in the sky has gone for ever. And this time, spreads the heavenly hedgerow rumour, it is the Earth. The Earth has killed itself. It is black, petrified, wizened, poisoned, burst; insanity has blown it rotten; and no creatures at all, joyful, despairing, cruel, kind, dumb, afire, loving, dull, shortly and brutishly hunt their days down like enemies on that corrupted face. And, one by one, those heavenly hedgerow-men who once were of the Earth call to one another, through the long night, Light and His tears falling, what they remember, what they sense in the submerged wilderness and on the exposed hair's breadth of the mind, what they feel trembling on the nerves of a nerve, what they know in their Edenie hearts, of that self-called place. They remember places, fears, loves, exultation, misery, animal joy, ignorance, and mysteries, all *we* know and do not know.

The poem is made of these tellings. And the poem becomes, at last, an affirmation of the beautiful and terrible worth of the Earth. It grows into a praise of what is and what could be on this lump in the skies. It is a poem about happiness.[35]

This long statement reveals, beneath the typical exuberance and verve of its prose, that Thomas understood the nature of his poetry better than some of his critics. It is, as I have said before, essentially a religious poetry, and a poetry which combines a tragic vision with a sense of joy. Nowhere is this more apparent than in these last poems. (Two of Thomas's Welsh critics, Aneirin Talfan Davies and Raymond Garlick, have pointed to an increasing use of Catholic imagery in his poetry from *Deaths and Entrances* onwards, though neither of them is able to say just how much importance we should attach to this.) "In Country Sleep" is the most visionary of his poems. Its theme is simple enough: the poet is expressing his love and care for a small girl, presumably his daughter, telling her not to fear the creatures of the imagination, "the wolf in a sheep-white hood," "no gooseherd or swine," "nor the tusked prince." "Yet," he tells her, "out of the beaked, web dark and the pouncing boughs | Be you sure the Thief will seek a way sly and sure." This capitalised Thief is obviously God, the bringer of death ("But the day of the Lord will come as a thief in the night; in the which the heavens shall pass away with a great noise, and the elements shall melt with fervent heat, the earth also and the works that are therein shall be burned up.")[36] This is all that is to be feared "in country sleep," but meanwhile

> The country is holy: O bide in that country kind,
> > Know the green good, . . .[37]

The second part of the poem is an exultantly lyrical celebration of the night itself as the girl lies sleeping:

> Night and the vein of birds in the winged, sloe wrist
>   of the wood![38]

and the fact that, so long as she keeps faith, although God comes to her every night as she lies "in country sleep," he has not yet come to her in the guise of the Thief, as death.

Ever and ever by all your vows believe and fear
My dear this night he comes and night without end
    my dear
                        Since you were born:
And you shall wake, from country sleep, this dawn
    and each first dawn,
Your faith as deathless as the outcry of the ruled sun.[39]

The poem is remarkable for its combination of tender
feeling and elaborate construction.

Equally formal and elaborate is "Over Sir John's Hill."
This poem, as Elder Olson has shown, is really an expanded metaphor: the gallows and tyburn of the first
stanza are there because in the second stanza Sir John's
hill is just, that is, it does justice, and it does this because it
puts on a black cap (of jackdaws). If it were no more than
this, the poem would be merely an ingenious and fantastic
conceit; but it is much more than this. It is, partly,
another visionary poem: this time, the poet's vision is of
the tragic order of the natural world.

I open the leaves of the water at a passage
Of psalms and shadows among the pincered sand-
    crabs prancing
And read, in a shell,
Death clear as a buoy's bell. . . .[40]

And it is also the poet's intercessionary prayer in his dual
role as visionary witness and trumpet-tongued celebrator
for this doomed and guilty order of the fallen world:

        and I who hear the tune of the slow,
Wear-willow river, grave,
Before the lunge of the night, the notes on this time-
    shaken
Stone for the sake of the souls of the slain birds
    sailing.[41]

"In the white Giant's Thigh" (the title is taken from

the name of a hill in the Dylan Thomas country) is a celebration of sexual love, of Hamlet's "country matters." Its narrative thread is given in the opening lines:

> I walk in the white giant's thigh
> Where barren as boulders women lie longing still
>
> To labour and love though they lay down long ago.[42]

and in the three lines printed singly at strategic intervals through the rest of the poem:

> Who once, green countries since, were a hedgerow
> of joys. . . .
>
> Now curlew cry me down to kiss the mouths of their
> dust. . . .
>
> And the daughters of darkness flame like Fawkes
> fires still. . . .[43]

Since Thomas has so often been accused of, or praised for, writing about "birth, copulation, and death," it is an interesting demonstration to compare his treatment of sexual love in this poem (and for that matter, in "Lament," too) with its treatment in an early poem like "If I were Tickled by the Rub of Love." There it had been:

> This world is half the devil's and my own,
> Daft with the drug that's smoking in a girl
> And curling round the bud that forks her eye.[44]

Now it is:

> or gay with any one
> Young as they in the after milking moonlight lay
>
> . . . a bloom of wayside brides in the hawed
> house. . . .
>
> Or, butter fat goosegirls, bounced in a gambo bed,
> Their breasts full of honey. . . .[45]

What had been an adolescent torment, horrifiedly seen in ineluctable relation to disease, decay, and death, is now one of the "tellings" or affirmations "of the beautiful and terrible worth of the Earth."

These three poems also show a further development of something that had become apparent in *Deaths and Entrances*: the poet's increasing ability to stand away from and outside his own self and problems, and to write objectively. It is true that all three are spoken by a first-person narrator, and that this narrator may fairly be taken to be the poet himself; but it is the poet in his role as poet, as the equivalent of the anonymous, unjudging First Voice of *Under Milk Wood*, witness and celebrator, not the poet of *18 Poems* obsessed with his own guilts and failures and the twin torments of sex and death.

Of the other poems of his last years, two, "Author's Prologue" and "Poem on his Birthday" are, of course, self-centred; and two, "Do not go Gentle into that Good Night" and the unfinished "Elegy" are addressed to his father. In "Do not go Gentle," written at a time when his father was seriously ill, Thomas used the difficult villanelle form which he had previously employed in his parodic "Homage to William Empson." Empson had already demonstrated that the villanelle could be used in English for serious poetic purposes: Thomas had always been concerned, even obsessed, with the challenge of form, had always sought to give his poems "imposed formal limits." In this poem he achieves the seemingly impossible, using the highly contrived form of the villanelle not merely to make poetry that has seriousness, but poetry that has pathos also:

> Do not go gentle into that good night,
> Old age should burn and rave at close of day;
> Rage, rage against the dying of the light.[46]

The combination of the artifice of the form and the

passionate, monosyllabic simplicity of the words make this one of Thomas's most moving poems. When his father died in 1952, he wrote simply in reply to a letter from Vernon Watkins, "Thank you so much. I miss him a great deal."[47] Among his papers Thomas left sixty pages of manuscript work towards an elegy on his father, and from these notes and drafts Vernon Watkins extended and built up a complete poem which cannot be far from what would have been Thomas's final version. In the villanelle, the motivating force of the poem had been the poet's wish that his father should not die. In "Elegy," the emphasis is on the father himself:

> Too proud to die, broken and blind he died
> The darkest way, and did not turn away,
> A cold kind man brave in his narrow pride
>
> On that darkest day.[48]

Again as in the villanelle we have a combination of formal artifice and an almost primitive simplicity of emotion expressed mainly in monosyllables; and as Watkins says in his note to the poem, while it recalls the earlier poem, "it is clear that in this last poem Dylan Thomas was attempting something even more immediate and more difficult." In these two poems, and particularly in the "Elegy," unfinished as he left it, it seems to me that Thomas achieved a purity of expression heightened by a ceremonious formality that makes them outstanding among the poems of our time.

> The rivers of the dead
> Veined his poor hand I held, and I saw
> Through his unseeing eyes to the roots of the sea. . . .
>
> Until I die he will not leave my side.[49]

In "Poem on his Birthday" (first published in 1951 but

written in celebration of his thirty-fifth birthday in 1949)
Thomas for the last time dealt with a theme that had
preoccupied him since he was a very young poet: the
inexorable progress of time and onset of age as these are
marked out for a man by the succession of his birthdays,
each "a year to heaven." Because Thomas died so soon
after the publication of this poem it is all too easy to see
in its last line—

> As I sail out to die

—an echo of D. H. Lawrence's "The Ship of Death"
(particularly since we know that he admired Lawrence's
poems), and so, by extrapolation, to read the poem as
Thomas's anticipation of his own more or less immediate
death. But, as we have seen, Thomas had been antici-
pating his own death practically all his life. The first birthday poem he had written had ended:

> Dressed to die, the sensual strut begun,
> With my red veins full of money,
> In the final direction of the elementary town
> I advance for as long as forever is.[50]

In his last birthday poem, expressions like "the closer I
move | To death" and "As I sail out to die" may surely be
taken literally, as the poet once said all his poetry should
be—they imply no more than, that as a man grows older,
the closer he is to death. Once we recognise and admit
this, we can see that the poem is fundamentally one more
of Thomas's exultant, celebratory pieces. It is indeed his
most triumphant poem, the one in which what D. C.
Muecke has called "his love of the multitudinary world"[51]
is most affirmatively expressed.

> And this last blessing most,
>
> That the closer I move
> To death, one man through his sundered hulks,

The louder the sun blooms
And the tusked, ramshackling sea exults; . . .

I hear the bouncing hills
Grow larked and greener at berry brown
    Fall and the dew larks sing
Taller this thunderclap spring, and how
    More spanned with angels ride
The mansouled fiery islands! Oh,
    Holier then their eyes,
And my shining men no more alone
    As I sail out to die.[52]

The "Author's Prologue" written especially for
Collected Poems in 1952 is another affirmation of Thomas's
vision and faith. And here, for the first time, he explicitly
wove together most of the dominant strands of his creative
output: the world of nature, Wales, the concept of poetry
itself, the sense of glory.

. . . I, a spinning man,
Glory also this star, bird
Roared, sea born, man torn, blood blest. . . .

We will ride out alone, and then,
Under the stars of Wales,
Cry, Multitudes of arks! . . .

My ark sings in the sun
At God speeded summer's end
And the flood flowers now.[53]

In October 1953, only a few months after his first
public reading there of *Under Milk Wood*, Thomas
returned to America for his fourth and last visit. According to Brinnin's account, he was a very sick man from the
day of his arrival; and in November he died. At the time
of his death, he was perhaps the most notorious poet in

H

the world; he was also, we might notice, a decade younger than Yeats was when he asked pardon of his old fathers because he had nothing but a book, "Nothing but that to prove your blood and mine."[54]

Various people, including some who should have known better, have suggested that in these last years of Thomas's life there was a failing of his poetic powers. The springs of his inspiration, it is suggested, were drying up—his awareness of this drove him further and more desperately along his self-chosen, self-destructive path. Even more ridiculously, the extreme exponents of this view hint or state that had he lived (managing in an established way to suggest that somehow it was a good thing for him and for us that he did not, that his death— naturally without a whisper of blasphemy—was a sort of fortunate fall, a *felix, mea non, culpa*) he would not have been a lyrical poet any longer, but a purveyor of more and more entertainment. Hypothetical argument or assertion one way or the other about such matters is futile; but the reader who comes to Thomas's last poems without a preconceived determination to find a death-wish in a man who died is more than likely to read them as the final flowering of Thomas's genius and to regret that untimely death.

Of his poems we may say that even the least intelligible appear to be communicating something, and that there is a definite, constant effort on the poet's part towards greater clarity and intelligibility. One of the best summaries of Thomas's obvious technical procedures is that given by David Aivaz:

The transition from image to image is by means of the pun, the double meaning, the coined word, the composite word, the noun-verb, the pronoun with a double antecedent. And there is a larger machinery, verbal and syntactical: clauses that read both forward and backward; uneven images that are smoothed by in-

cantatory rhythms, rhymes, word patterns, verse forms,
by the use of commas in place of full-stop punctuation;
cant, slang terms and formal, general abstract wording
juxtaposed in image after image, so that the agitation
of each becomes the repose of the group.[55]

Even this list by no means exhausts Thomas's devices.
We can usefully add to it some of the terms in Olson's
chapter, "Techniques of Depiction." According to this,
one of Thomas's general devices is "pseudo-drama . . .
the use of dialogue to suggest that the action represented
is the interplay among several distinct persons, whereas
in fact there is no such interplay because the 'persons' of
the dialogue are not distinct."[56] Pseudo-narrative is the
narrative parallel to this. Another "fairly constant, and
quite peculiar characteristic" which Olson finds in
Thomas's poetry is what he calls "circumstantial ambi-
guity." This refers to the "curious difficulty, as one first
approaches his poetry, of determining who is saying what
or doing what to whom in what circumstances. . . ."[57]
   In a letter to Henry Treece, Thomas said that much of
the obscurity of his poems was "due to rigorous compres-
sion; the last thing they do is to flow; they are much
rather hewn."[58] (The concept recurs in "Author's
Prologue" where he says "as I hack | This rumpus of
shapes" and "my flood ship's | Clangour as I hew and
smite," and in "Poem on his Birthday," where he refers
to "the hewn coils of his trade.") One aspect of his
development as a poet is the change from rigorous com-
pression to a more expansive mode; from:

> And from the windy West came two-gunned Gabriel,
> From Jesu's sleeve trumped up the king of spots,
> The sheath-decked jacks, queen with a shuffled heart;
> Said the fake gentleman in suit of spades,
> Black-tongued and tipsy from salvation's bottle.
> Rose my Byzantine Adam in the night. . . .[59]

to:

>   Earth, air, water, fire, singing into the white act,
>
>   The haygold haired, my love asleep, and the rift blue
>   Eyed, in the haloed house, in her rareness and hilly
>   High riding, held and blessed and true, and so stilly
>   Lying the sky
>   Might cross its planets, the bell weep, night gather
>   her eyes,
>   The Thief fall on the dead like the willy nilly dew,
>
>   Only for the turning of the earth in her holy Heart![60]

In an interesting study of Thomas's stylistic development, William T. Moynihan finds that

> The principal direction of Thomas' intonational de-
> velopment is from a poetry of strong metrical stress to a
> poetry of flowing cadence. Accompanying this shift,
> and perhaps the cause of it, is a change from a highly
> specific, involved imagery to a more general, obvious
> imagery.[61]

Accompanying these technical changes there was also, as
we have seen, a development in Thomas's poetry which
may be characterised as both an increasing awareness of
his own human nature and a growing ability to present
the human nature of other people. It might very well be,
as Fraser suggests, that towards the end of his life the two
main elements of Thomas's complexity, "the legendary
sweet funny man and the fine solemn poet, were growing
together"; at least, there is more evidence in the work
itself for this than for the alternative hypothesis of failing
powers and a wish for death.

Thomas received in his lifetime a great deal of extrava-
gant and often unintelligent praise. The adverse criticism
that he received came from an odd assortment of people:
James Agate of the *Daily Express* and other professional

Philistines, very old-fashioned lovers of old-fashioned poetry, Mr Geoffrey Grigson, and the writers for *Scrutiny*. Of these, only the last two need be taken in any way seriously. Grigson's attack is summed up in the following statement:

> *Deaths and Entrances* shows, not a theme, not medita-tion, but simply obsession;—obsession with birth, death, and love, and obsession mainly in a muddle of images with only the frailest ineptitude of structure.[62]

Why an obsession with birth, death, and love should be a fault in a poet is not made clear—most poets have taken it to be an inevitability and, at the worst, have made a virtue from necessity. The second part of Grigson's charge is more important. Particularly in the early poems of Thomas the imagery is sometimes muddled:

> Sir morrow at his sponge,
> (The wound records),
> The nurse of giants by the cut sea basin,
> (Fog by his spring
> Soaks up the sewing tides),
> Tells you and you, my masters, as his strange
> Man morrow blows through food.[63]

—but, even in the early poems, such lapses are rare; and there is a demonstrable progress in Thomas's work towards greater coherence and clarity of imagery. As for Grigson's accusation of "formal awkwardness," one can only say that even the examples he gives show that Thomas is not guilty. Practically every critic who has bothered to analyse a poem by Thomas in detail has drawn attention to Thomas's technical skill, and in particular to his command of structure. And the number of contemporary poets, themselves very cunning crafts-men, who have paid tribute to Thomas's technique, is large: among others Vernon Watkins, Roy Campbell, Theodore Roethke, W. S. Merwin. (Robert Graves is an outstanding exception, but his opinions about other poets are notably eccentric.)

Grigson's attack on what he saw as the weaknesses of Thomas's poetry was really an attack on a short-lived and somewhat amorphous literary movement loosely called neo-romanticism, a movement which Thomas did not invent and for which he cannot, in fairness, be held responsible. Critics like Wolf Mankowitz and David Holbrook have no such excuse. In *Scrutiny* (Summer, 1946) Mankowitz said "Mr Thomas does not offer very much to the literary critic for analysis," having previously demonstrated his own incapacity for critical analysis. A more recent example of critical ineptitude passing itself off as critical superiority is provided by David Holbrook's incredible essay in Vol. VII of *The Pelican Guide to English Literature*. The uninformed reader would gather from this that Thomas's most important work was *Under Milk Wood* (which isn't much good), and that he wrote a few unsuccessful poems which are scarcely worth talking about.

Thomas has also suffered from his admirers. Apart from a great deal of enthusiastic nonsense which may be found in the files of little magazines, there are the first two books on Thomas, one by Henry Treece and one by Derek Stanford. Both of these were premature and unworthy of their subject. On the other hand, there have been a number of intelligent and perceptive studies of Thomas, most of which I have quoted or referred to in this book. Elder Olson's book, though I think it makes exaggerated claims for the sonnets, is an illuminating study of the poetry, and G. S. Fraser's pamphlet is the best brief introduction to the whole of Thomas's work.

One of Thomas's best-known poems is "In my Craft or Sullen Art." Because, presumably, of its popularity, this lyric has been treated, even by some appreciative critics, as if it were Thomas's party piece, his equivalent of Yeats's "The Lake Isle of Innisfree." There is no warrant for this, either in the poem itself or in Thomas's attitude towards it. It is, in fact, a central poem in Thomas's work: a poem which says, clearly and beautifully, what the whole of his work says, and a poem where our appreciation of his genius must begin:

> Not for the proud man apart
> From the raging moon I write
> On these spindrift pages
> Nor for the towering dead
> With their nightingales and psalms
> But for the lovers, their arms
> Round the griefs of the ages,
> Who pay no praise or wages
> Nor heed my craft or art.[64]

For genius he was. He was not a major poet; but he was a good poet. Now that more than a decade has passed since he died, and the fuss about his life and death becomes more and more remotely gossipy and unimportant, his work stays more and more firmly in the minds of those who care for poetry.

The true Thomas was not the anti-hero of a thousand sniggered tales, nor the retching wreck eventually passing into oblivion in a New York hospital, but the author of "Fern Hill" and "A Refusal to Mourn" and twenty or thirty other equally fine poems, of stories like "The Peaches" and "A Visit to Grandpa's," and of *Under Milk Wood*, and the man who was loved by his parents, his wife, and his friends. One could not end a book on him more fittingly than by quoting a poem written to him by one of those friends, Vernon Watkins:

> He has sent me this
> Late and early page. . . .
>
> Who for annunciation has
> The white wings of the sheldrake
> Labouring water's praise, . . .

Toiling, as with closed eyes,
Love's language to remake, . . .

Trusting a creaking house,
His roof is ruinous,
So mortal. A real wind
Beats on this house of sand
Two tides like ages buffet.
The superhuman, crowned
Saints must enter this drowned
Tide-race of the mind
To guess or understand
The face of this cracked prophet,
Which from its patient pall
I slowly take,
Drop the envelope,
Compel his disturbing shape,
And write these words on a wall
Maybe for a third man's sake.[65]

REFERENCES

1. *C.P.*, p. vii.
2. *New World Writing. Seventh Mentor Selection*, p. 129.
3. Brinnin, *Dylan Thomas in America*, p. v.
4. *Q.E.O.M.*, p. 131.
5. *Op. cit.*, pp. 174-5.
6. *Op. cit.*, p. 16.
7. *Op. cit.*, p. 47.
8. Brinnin, *Dylan Thomas in America*, p. 20.
9. *Q.E.O.M.*, p. 20.
10. *Op. cit.*, p. 31.
11. *New World Writing. Seventh Mentor Edition*, p. 128.
12. Derek Stanford, *Dylan Thomas*, London 1954, pp. 177-9.
13. *Poetry (Chicago)*, LXXXVII (1955-6), 116.
14. *D.D.*, p. 2.
15. *Ibid.*, p. 2.
16. *D.D.*, p. 89.
17. *D.D.*, p. 37.
18. Richard Hughes, in a letter to the author.
19. *Q.E.O.M.*, p. x.
20. *Botteghe Oscure*, No. XIII (Apr. 1953), 93-102.
21. Brinnin, *Dylan Thomas in America*, p. 152.
22. Stanford, *Dylan Thomas*, pp. 181-2.
23. David Holbrook, "Metaphor and Maturity: T. F. Powys and Dylan

Thomas," in *The Pelican Guide to English Literature*, VII (Harmondsworth 1961), 417.

24. *Q.E.O.M.*, p. 17.
25. *U.M.W.*, p. 70.
26. *Op. cit.*, p. 42.
27. Richard Hughes, in a letter to the author.
28. *Q.E.O.M.*, p. 20.
29. *U.M.W.*, p. 54.
30. *Botteghe Oscure*, No. XIII (Apr. 1953), pp. 93–102.
31. *U.M.W.*, pp. 24, 79.
32. Holbrook, "Metaphor and Maturity . . . ," in *The Pelican Guide to English Literature*, VII. 417.
33. *U.M.W.*, p. v.
34. *Adam International Review*, 238 (1953), 36–7.
35. *Q.E.O.M.*, pp. 156–7.
36. II Pet. III. 10.
37. *C.P.*, p. 163.
38. *C.P.*, p. 164.
39. *C.P.*, p. 166.
40. *C.P.*, pp. 167–8.
41. *C.P.*, p. 169.
42. *C.P.*, p. 176.
43. *C.P.*, pp. 176, 178.
44. *C.P.*, p. 13.
45. *C.P.*, pp. 176, 177.
46. *C.P.*, p. 116.
47. *Letters*, p. 140.
48. *Encounter*, VI (1956), 30–1; *New Poems, 1956*, pp. 60–62.
49. *Loc. cit.*
50. *C.P.*, p. 99.
51. Muecke, " 'Come back! Come back!', A Theme in Dylan Thomas's Prose," in *Meanjin*, XVIII (1959), 69–76.
52. *C.P.*, p. 173.
53. *C.P.*, pp. viii, x.
54. W. B. Yeats, *Collected Poems*, 2nd edn, London 1950, p. 113.
55. David Aivaz, "The Poetry of Dylan Thomas," in Tedlock, pp. 190–1.
56. Olson, *The Poetry of Dylan Thomas*, p. 42.
57. Olson, *op. cit.*, p. 45.
58. Treece, *Dylan Thomas*, pp. 141–2.
59. "Sonnet V," in *C.P.*, p. 73.
60. "In Country Sleep," in *C.P.*, p. 165.
61. William T. Moynihan, "Dylan Thomas' 'Hewn Voice'," in *Texas Studies in Language and Literature*, I (1959), 42.
62. Grigson, "How Much Me Now Your Acrobatics Amaze," in Tedlock, p. 160.
63. *C.P.*, p. 56.
64. *C.P.*, p. 128.
65. *Letters*, pp. 34–5; repr. in Vernon Watkins, *The Ballad of the Mari Lwyd*, pp. 36–8.

BIBLIOGRAPHY

BIBLIOGRAPHY

I. DYLAN THOMAS

Only his principal works are here listed.

18 Poems. London (The Parton Bookshop) 1934.

Twenty-five Poems. London (Dent) 1936.

The Map of Love. London (Dent) 1939.

The World I Breathe. Norfolk, Conn. (New Directions) 1939.

Portrait of the Artist as a Young Dog. London (Dent) 1940; New York (New Directions) 1956.

Deaths and Entrances. London (Dent) 1946.

Collected Poems. London (Dent) 1952; New York (New Directions) 1952.

The Doctor and the Devils. London (Dent) 1953.

Under Milk Wood. London (Dent) 1954; New York (New Directions) 1959.

Quite Early one Morning. London (Dent) 1954; New York (New Directions) 1954.

A Prospect of the Sea. London (Dent) 1955.

Adventures in the Skin Trade. London (Putnam) 1955; New York (New Directions) 1955.

Letters to Vernon Watkins. London (Dent/Faber) 1957; New York (New Directions) 1957.

Child's Christmas in Wales (rev. ed.) New York (New Directions) 1959.

II. OTHERS

BAYLEY, JOHN: *The Romantic Survival.* London and New York 1957.

BRINNIN, JOHN MALCOLM: *Dylan Thomas in America.* London 1956; Boston, Mass., 1955.

DAVIES, ANEIRIN TALFAN: "A Question of Language," in *Yr Einion*, v (1953), 19ff.

Dylan Thomas: The Legend and the Poet, ed. E. W. Tedlock. London 1960. Contains all important articles on Thomas not separately listed here.

FRASER, G. S.: *Dylan Thomas.* In "Writers and their Work." London (Longmans) and New York 1957.

GARLICK, RAYMOND: "The Endless Breviary," in *The Month*, CXCVII (1954), pp. 143ff.

HOLBROOK, DAVID: *Llareggub Revisited: Dylan Thomas and the state of modern poetry.* Cambridge 1962.

HUDDLESTONE, LINDEN: "An Approach to Dylan Thomas," in *Penguin New Writing*, 35 (1948), 123 ff.

JONES, GWYN: "Welsh Dylan," in *The Adelphi*, XXX (1954), 108ff.

LEWIS, E. GLYN: "Some Aspects of Anglo-Welsh Literature," in *The Welsh Review*, V (1946), pp. 176ff.

MAUD, R. N.: "Dylan Thomas's Poetry," in *Essays in Criticism*, IV (1954), 411ff.

MELCHIORI, GEORGIO: *The Tight-Rope Walkers*, London and New York 1956.

MUECKE, D. C.: " 'Come back! Come back!' A Theme in Dylan Thomas's Prose," in *Meanjin*, XVIII (1959), 69 ff.

OLSON, ELDER: *The Poetry of Dylan Thomas*. Chicago 1954.

ROLPH, J. A.: *Dylan Thomas: A Bibliography*. London 1956.

STANFORD, DEREK: *Dylan Thomas*. London 1954.

TREECE, HENRY: *Dylan Thomas*, London 1949; New York 1956.